NIẒĀM-E-NAU

NEW WORLD ORDER OF ISLAM

by

ḤAḌRAT MIRZĀ BASHĪRUDDĪN MAḤMŪD AḤMAD[ra]
(Khalīfatul Masīḥ II)
The Second Successor of the Promised Messiah[as]

2005
ISLAM INTERNATIONAL PUBLICATIONS LIMITED

نظام نو

(Niẓām-e-Nau)
THE NEW WORLD ORDER OF ISLAM

A lecture delivered in Urdu in 1942 by Ḥaḍrat Mirzā Bashīruddīn Maḥmūd Aḥmad Khalīfatul Masīḥ II[ra]

Translated into English by Sir Muhammad Zafrullah Khan, assisted by Q. M. Aslam
Present edition edited by Mirzā Anas Aḥmad, M. A. M. Litt. (OXON)

© Islam International Publications Ltd

Editions
First published in Urdu 1943
Reprinted in 1944, 1945
Several Editions Published since
First English Edition Published in 1946
Reprinted in 1961, 1969
First Published in England 2005

Published by
Islam International Publications Ltd
Islamabad
Sheephatch Lane
Tilford, Surrey
United Kingdom GU10 2AQ

Printed in UK at
Raqeem Press
Tilford, Surrey

ISBN: 1 85372 754 7

Contents

ABOUT THE AUTHOR I
NOTE BY THE TRANSLATOR V
PREFACE TO THE FIRST EDITION VII
PREFACE TO THE SECOND EDITION XI
FOREWORD TO THE PRESENT EDITION XIII
CONTENTS OF THE BOOK.. XVIII
NEW WORLD ORDER 1-141
GLOSSARY 143
ANALYTICAL INDEX 145

ABOUT THE AUTHOR

The Promised son[ra] of the Promised Messiah and Mahdi[as]; the manifest Sign of Allah, the Almighty; the Word of God whose advent was prophesied by the Holy Prophet Muhammad[sa] and the Promised Messiah[as] as well as the past Prophets; a Star in the spiritual firmament for the like of which the world has to wait for hundreds of years to appear; the man of God, crowned with a spiritual hallo from which radiated such scintillating rays of light as would instil spiritual life into his followers and captivate and enthral those who were not fortunate to follow him; an orator of such phenomenal quality that his speeches would make his audience stay put for hours on end, come rain or shine, deep into the late hours of the evenings while words flowed from his tongue like honey dripping into their ears to reach the depths of their soul to fill them with knowledge and invigorate their faith; the ocean of Divine and secular knowledge; the Voice Articulate of the age; without doubt the greatest genius of the 20th century; a man of phenomenal intelligence and memory; an epitome of the qualities of leadership; the one whose versatility cannot be comprehended—Ḥaḍrat Mirzā Bashīruddīn Maḥmūd Aḥmad[ra] (1889-1965), *Muṣliḥ Mauʿūd* (the Promised Reformer) was the eldest son and the second successor (Khalīfa) of the Promised Messiah[as]. He took charge of the *Aḥmadiyya Jamāʿat* at the young age of 24 when the *Jamāʿat* was still in its infancy and nourished it to its maturity for more than 50 years with his spiritual guidance, prayers, tears, toil and blood. Not only did he fortify the foundations of the community laid down by the Promised Messiah[as], but expanded the structure of the *Jamāʿat* by initiating various schemes, organizations, and programs taking his inspiration from the Promised Messiah[as] and under the Divine guidance. His foremost concern, to which he devoted all his life, was to accomplish the mission of the Promised Messiah—the daunting task of spreading the message of true Islam in its pristine purity to the ends of the world. To achieve this, he initiated *Taḥrīk-e-Jadīd* through which spread, and continues to spread, the missionary work all over the globe. His acute intelligence, keen intellect, deep and extensive scholarship and above all his God-given knowledge enabled him to produce a vast corpus of writings, speeches etc. His oeuvre is so vast that it will take many years to see the light of publication.

When the promised Messiah[as] fervently prayed to God to grant him a Sign in support of Islam, Allah gave him the good tiding about this son of his and said:

"…He will be extremely intelligent … and will be filled with secular and spiritual knowledge … Son, delight of the heart, high ranking, noble; a manifestation of the First and the Last, of the True and the High; as if Allah has descended from heaven. Behold a light cometh. We shall pour our spirit into him…" [Revelation of 20th February 1886][*]

---

[*] Translation from Urdu by Sir Muḥammad Ẓafrullāh Khān in his English translation of Tadhkira—the book containing dreams, visions and verbal revelations vouchsafed to the Promised Messiah[as]. The book containing dreams, visions and verbal revelations vouchsafed to the Promised Messiah[as]. [Publisher]

NOTE BY THE TRANSLATOR

In delivering a speech, the speaker has often to repeat his points in order to impress them upon his audience. The same may, to some extent, be necessary when the speech or its translation has to be published, but not to the extent to which it seems necessary while speaking. I have, therefore, omitted repetitions which might have appeared wearisome to the reader. I have also, for the sake of idiom, occasionally departed from the literal text while preserving or explaining the sense. In one or two places I have omitted illustrations.

PREFACE TO THE FIRST EDITION

HERE follows the English version of an address, delivered by the late Amīrul-Mu'minīn,[*] Ḥaḍrat Mirzā Bashīruddīn Maḥmūd Aḥmad, to the Aḥmadiyya Annual Gathering on December 28, 1942.

A verbatim Urdu report of the original was issued in December, 1943, and again in April, 1944, and in March, 1945.

The English version is being issued to give wider publicity to the important subject matter of the address.

The address answers the question—'How does Aḥmadiyyat, the True Islam, propose to deal with the problem of social inequality in the world?' The Aḥmadiyya solution is the solution of Islam shaped under divine guidance for present needs by the Holy Founder[as] of the Aḥmadiyya Movement. It builds on Islamic teaching and emphasises the progressive nature of that teaching.

The social teaching of Islam[**] was expounded by

---

[*] The Leader or Imam of the faithful (publisher)
[**] A lecture on *The Economic Structure of Islamic Society*, delivered by the *Amīrul-Mu'minīn* at Lahore, has already been published. It can be had from the Oriental Religious Publishing Corporation Ltd., Rabwah, Pakistan.

the Amīrul Mu'minīn himself in 1924 in his *Ahmadiyyat or the True Islam*, and has since become wellknown. It consists of the statutory prohibition of interest, the tax of Zakat and the division of inheritances. It also includes general instructions regarding voluntary contributions by individuals which leaders of Islam from the earliest times have organised in different ways and devoted to the service of society.

The Holy Founder of the Ahmadiyya Movement[as] (d. 1908) instituted among his followers a system of voluntary consecration of properties by individual Ahmadīs to the needs of Islam in the widest sense of the term. The institution was promulgated by him in his *Al-Wasiyyat* (The Will) in 1905, and since then willing away portions of properties and income to the Central Anjuman-e-Ahmadiyya at Qādiān have become a common practice with Ahmadīs.

The Amīrul Mū'minīn announced in his address that the social order of Islam, built on the pillars of its economic teachings, would continue to grow. It would grow through *Al-Wasiyyat,* the institution of willing away properties and income; inaugurated by the Founder of Ahmadiyyat[as] in 1905. The institution of *Al-Wasiyyat,* therefore, answers the question which

---

(This lecture expounds in details Islamic economic system whereas the subject is only succinctly dealt in the *Ahmadiyyat or the True Islam.*)
[Publisher of the present edition]

many Muslims and non-Muslims seem to be asking today: 'Is Islam progressive?' It also answers the wider question 'Is religion progressive?'

The Ahmadiyya solution of the problem of inequality, it is as well to say, will, spread in the world at the rate at which Ahmadiyyat spreads. The pace cannot be forced, as Ahmadiyyat is obliged under Islamic teachings to use only one method for its propagation—the method of argument and honest conviction. Those, who accept the general principle of this solution but think its establishment throughout the world will take too long, can assist in the solution by applying its principles in their own way.

Until, however, the scheme of *Al-Waṣiyyat* becomes reasonably effective, another scheme known as the *Tahrīk-e-Jadīd* (The New Scheme) will take its place. This scheme was announced by the Amīrul Mu'minīn in a series of Friday sermons in 1934. Its nineteen clauses may be summarised as an organised effort for the promotion of discipline, simplicity and voluntary sacrifice by the members for the conservation of a Central Fund, devoted ultimately to strengthening and promoting the work which Ahmadiyyat is doing for the spread of Islam and its institutions.

The *Tahrīk-e-Jadīd*, therefore, is a forerunner of the New World Order of Islam and is intimately connected with it. This is why the address begins and ends by references to it.

M. Aslam

for the Publisher.

Qādiān, 1946.

PREFACE TO THE SECOND EDITION

The first English Edition of "The New World Order of Islam" was published in 1946.

Its Turkish translation was first printed in 1959. It was revised and reprinted in 1968.

The author, the late Ḥaḍrat Mirzā Bashīr-ud-Dīn Maḥmūd Aḥmad, Khalīfatul Masīḥ II (May God be pleased with him) has discussed the same theme in another booklet also, entitled, *The Economic Structure of Islamic Society*.

Both the publications supplement each other in evaluating the comparative worth of Communism, Capitalism and Islam in removing the economic ills of mankind;

Mirzā Mubārak Aḥmad
Wakīl-ut-Tabshīr.

FOREWORD TO THE PRESENT EDITION

In the backdrop of the then prevailing ideologies of communism and capitalist democracy, the second successor of the Ahmadiyya Movement, Hadrat Mirzā Bashīruddīn Mahmūd Ahmad[ra], addressed this lecture to the Ahmadiyya Annual Gathering on December 28, 1942. The address answers the question, 'How does Ahmadiyyat, the True Islam, propose to deal with the grave problem of socio-economic inequality in the world?' The Ahmadiyya solution is the solution of Islam shaped under divine guidance for present needs by the Holy Founder[as] of the Ahmadiyya movement.

The social and economic differences between the haves and the havenots are not only being intensified but are also being more and more bitterly felt. That with progress in every walk of life the disparities would reduce and ultimately disappear was the hope of many which has not been realised. The speaker examines and analyses the role played by different movements to alleviate poverty and sufferings, such as, Socialism, International Socialism, Marxism, Bolshevism, Nazism and Fascism and so on. Because each one of these had drawbacks and defects it was bound to fail and so it happened. Each one of these movements either sought preferential or limited benefits or discriminated between classes which resulted in propagation of adversity or reduced human calibre to manual labour, resulting in the loss of intellectual creative abilities and approach.

The speaker also, explores the major religions of the world regarding the basic question "social inequality a serious problem." In comparison to Islam, their teachings totally fail to address the problem; rather than providing a satisfactory solution to it, they aggravate it. "The system of Judaism" he observes, "is purely racial. There is nothing universal in it… It also lays down very harsh conditions which must be imposed upon nations opposed to it." About Christianity and Hinduism he observes, "The message of Christianity is that the Law is a curse. If the law is a curse then all that it ordains or prohibits must also be a curse… The Hindu religion by inculcating the doctrines of karma and transmigration of souls has completely barred the door of peace and progress upon mankind". The doctrine of discrimination between the castes in the Hindu society worsens the problem under discussion. Only Islamic teachings—moral, social and economic—can eradicate the socio-economic ills of the world and usher in peace, harmony, equality and justice.

Haḍrat Mirzā Ghulām Aḥmad, the Promised Messiah and Mahdi[as], the founder of Aḥmadiyya Muslim Jamāʿat, laid down the foundations of the New World Order, by initiating the scheme of *Waṣiyyat* based on Islamic teachings and under the Divine guidance in his book '*Al-Waṣiyyat*' written in 1905. Later in 1934 Haḍrat Mirzā Bashīruddīn Maḥmūd Aḥmad[ra] inaugurated *Tahrīk-e-Jadīd* to prepare the ground for the full implementation of the New World Order of the institution of *Waṣiyyat*. In the present lecture he elaborates the aims and objectives of *Tahrīk-e-Jadīd* and claims that the New World Order in all its aspects, economic, social and religious, as introduced by *Niẓām-e-Waṣiyyat*, will at the end prevail and a new and genuine revolution will take place.

Though the lecture was delivered in the early forties since when the world has changed so much that it seems to be quite different from what it was then, yet the central message and many details of the lecture are still relevant and shall remain so till the true message of Islam gains supremacy in the world and the world, having been convinced of the truth of it, enters the fold of Islam. Keeping this in mind we have given an analytical index, instead of conventional one, to help the reader have full grasp of the drift of the main argument of the lecture and to comprehend its basic thesis. The reader may go through the Analytical Index before reading the book.

The name of Muhammad[sa], the Holy Prophet of Islam, has been followed by the symbol [sa], which is an abbreviation for the salutation 'may peace and blessings of Allah be upon him.' The names of other prophets and messengers are followed by the symbol [as], an abbreviation for 'on whom be peace.' The actual salutations have not generally been set out in full, but they should nevertheless, be understood as being repeated in full in each case. The symbol [ra] is used with the name of the Disciples of the Holy Prophet[sa] and those of the Promised Messiah[as]. It stands for *Raḍī Allāhu 'anhu/'anhā/'anhum* (May Allah be pleased with him/with her/with them).

In transliterating Arabic words we have followed the following system adopted by the Royal Asiatic Society.

ا   at the beginning of a word, pronounced as *a, i, u* preceded by a very slight aspiration, like *h* in the English word 'honour'.

ث   *th*, pronounced like th in the English word 'thing'.

ح   *ḥ*, a guttural aspirate, stronger than h.

خ   *kh*, pronounced like the Scotch ch in 'loch'.

ذ   *dh*, pronounced like the English th in 'that'.

ص   *ṣ*, strongly articulated s.

ض   *ḍ*, similar to the English th in 'this'.

ط   *ṭ*, strongly articulated palatal t.

ظ   *ẓ*, strongly articulated z.

ع   ', a strong guttural, the pronunciation of which must be learnt by the ear.

غ   *gh*, a sound approached very nearly in the r *'grasseye'* in French, and in the German r. It requires the muscles of the throat to be in the 'gargling' position whilst pronouncing it.

ق   *q*, a deep guttural k sound.

ء   ', a sort of catch in the voice.

Short vowels are represented by *a* for ─ؔ─ (like *u* in 'bud'); *i* for ─ؚ─ (like *i* in 'bid'); u for ─ؙ─ (like *oo* in 'wood'); the long vowels by *ā* for ─ا─ or آ (like *a* in 'father'); *ī* for ی ─ؚ─ or ─ِ─ (like *ee* in 'deep'); *ai* for ی ─ؔ─ (like *i* in 'site')*; *ū* for و ─ؙ─ (like *oo* in 'root'); *au* for و ─ؔ─ (resembling *ou* in 'sound').

The consonants not included in the above list have the same phonetic value as in the principal languages of Europe.

We have not transliterated Arabic, Persian or Urdu and Hindi words which have become part of English language, e.g., Islam, Mahdi, Qur'an, Hijra, Ramadan, Rahman, Hadith, Zakat, ulema, umma, sunna, kafir, Hindu, Hinduism, karma etc.

For quotes straight commas (straight quotes) are used to differentiate them from the curved commas used in the system of transliteration, ' for ع, ' for ء. Commas as punctuation marks are used according to the normal usage.

The Publishers

---

* In Arabic words like شیخ (Shaikh) there is an element of diphthong which is missing when the word is pronounced in Urdu.

Contents

	Pages
Preliminary remarks—Taḥrīk-e-Jadīd and its collective significance—to fulfil a great Islamic purpose and strengthen the foundations of human society	1

I
Increasing social differences in the world—machinery—attempts to alleviate poverty—some intolerable examples	3

II
Democracy—Socialism—International Socialism—Marx and his three principles—Lenin—Bolsheviks and Mensheviks—Lenin and Martove	10

III
Six Principles of Bolshevism—their consequences	18

IV
Reactions to Bolshevism—Nazism, Fascism and Falangists—their respective methods of propaganda	23

V
Socialism favourable to British, French and American labour—two dangers of Socialism—lack of sympathy for others and irreligion	31

VI
Communism and its defects—against individual effort and initiative—uses violence and constraint—anti-religious—favours dictatorship—discourages intellectual progress—promotes class struggle—will have dangerous reactions in case of failure	34

VII
National Socialism and its defects—the present war and its consequences—Victory of the United Nations better for India—Bolshevik victory and its consequences	42

VIII
Religion and the Problem of Social inequality—Judaism—Christianity—Hinduism	48

IX
Unrivalled Teachings of Islam—slavery abolished—only defensive war allowed—human treatment meted out to prisoners of war—easy conditions of freedom—historical examples	57

X
Fundamentals of an Islamic League of Nations—Causes

	Pages
of failure of the European League	83

XI
Islamic Teachings to help the poor—laws of inheritance—hoarding banned—prohibition of interest—Zakat and voluntary charity—personal ownership—superiority over Bolshevik principles—capacity a form of capital—social inequality under Bolshevism—loss of brains to the nation—danger of rebellion ... 87

XII
Need of more funds for the State—Zakat not enough—nor partnership in profits—nor State-ownership—Hitlerain scheme of raising funds Bolshevik scheme—Islamic scheme ... 100

XIII
Islamic scheme described—ban on luxuries—voluntary as well as obligatory contributions to State funds—keeping intact individual initiative—value of voluntary contributions—example of early Islam ... 106

XIV
Applications of Islamic principles to meet new needs—proposed by the Founder of the Ahmadiyya Movement in his *Al-Waṣiyyat* and announced in 1905—Qur'an on voluntary contributions—how *Al-Waṣiyyat* proposes to raise funds for Islam—expenditure of these funds—difference between Bolshevik and *Al-Waṣiyyat* funds—*Al-Waṣiyyat* a peaceful revolution—voluntary transfer of properties to society—*Al-Waṣiyyat* at universal—steady surrender of properties in the Islamic World Order ... 117

XV
The Order founded in Qādiān in 1905—future assured by divine promise and divine support ... 131

XVI
The New Order foreshadowed in Tahrīk-e-Jadīd ... 136

XVII
Exhortation to the Jamā'at ... 138

NEW WORLD ORDER

SPECIAL features of the *Tahrīk-e-Jadīd* have been explained and dwelt upon separately on several occasions, but the collective importance of the *Tahrīk* has never before been put before the community. In fact, I myself have realized it only gradually. When I inaugurated the *Tahrīk-e-Jadīd* in my first address, its different features took shape in my mind, as it were, by divine inspiration, and I went on explaining them as I was inspired. The truth, therefore, is that many of its benefits and objects remained hidden even from me and I did not even realize all its implications. It may have been a part of the divine purpose that attention should be drawn to the collective importance of the *Tahrīk-e-Jadīd* only at a particular stage in its growth, and that may be the reason why attention has not so far been paid to it. However, there is no doubt now, that the *Tahrīk* has a universal aspect. It is necessary that this aspect should be explained.

What I propose to say, therefore, is that the *Tahrīk-e-Jadīd*, which I inaugurated some time ago under Divine inspiration, contains within it the seed which in due time will grow to fulfil a great Islamic purpose and serve to strengthen the foundations of human society.

As I proceed, you may begin to wonder, what connection the subject of my address has with the *Taḥrīk-e-Jadīd*. But if you are patient to the end and try to follow carefully what I have to say, you will realize the relevance it has to the *Taḥrīk-e-Jadīd*.

It is not possible to understand anything except in its own proper setting. Torn from its setting the most beautiful object loses its charm. Unless, therefore, I give you the setting of *Taḥrīk-e-Jadīd* you will not understand what it all is about. This is all the more necessary, because a large majority of the members of our *Jamā'at* belongs to rural areas, ill-acquainted with the thought movements of their day. This necessitates some explanation of the conditions through which mankind have passed recently, and which compelled me to inaugurate the *Taḥrīk*. I must also examine the changes which are going on around us and explain how they are likely to affect the future—particularly the future of our Movement, and other Muslim communities. If these changes in their operation are likely to prove injurious, what steps ought we to take to guard ourselves against them, and if beneficial, to what extent ought we to adopt them?

I

I must begin by telling you that the social and economic differences, which we observe today between the rich and the poor, the haves and the have-nots, are not only being intensified, but are also being more and more bitterly felt. Differences in wealth and worldly possessions have existed as far back as one can see, but the contrast was never as great as it is today. Big landlords, whose dues were collected in cash and kind, were in the habit of disbursing them back again among their tenants and dependants. This is still the case with some of those living in remote parts of the country. I remember, some years ago during one of my visits to Lahore, I heard of a big landholder of the Punjab lying ill there. I heard that during his illness he was being visited by hundreds of people from his part of the country. They came to inquire after his health. Every one of these visitors would bring a present for the ailing chief: sheep, a quantity of rice or some home-made sugar. The chief, on his side, had instituted a big kitchen and all these supplies were supplemented and utilized for feeding the string of visitors from the countryside. His illness lasted two or three months. So the arrangement continued during this time.

What I wish to say is that, in spite of differences in wealth, the wealthy were in the habit of using their goods and possessions in a manner which occasioned no resentment. Again, in the past the relation between the master and the servant was on a basis very different from that of today. In well-to-do families servants and dependants were treated as members of the household. Distinctions were no doubt maintained. For instance, a master would not marry his daughter to any of his servants, nor was it considered proper for the master himself to marry a servant girl. Nevertheless, the distance between the master and the servant was not so great, nor was it stressed so much as it is today. The master sat on the floor and his servants and dependants sat freely around him. The mistress and her serving women similarly spent their time freely together. Today the master sits on the chair and the servant must remain in attendance standing in a respectful attitude. However tired he may be, he dare not sit in the presence of the master. Even the new modes of travel serve to maintain and stress distinctions. In the past the master and the servant used to ride together across the country. No doubt the master was better mounted than the servant, but both rode together in companionship. Today while the master travels first or second among his own class, the servant travels among his fellows in the third class. Again, the residences of the rich and the poor today exhibit much more emphatically the difference between their conditions than they did in the past. So long as the principal article of furniture was carpets, however rich the stuff or varied the design, the poor could imitate the rich with cheap varieties of their own. Today furnishing and apartments have assumed a standard and a variety which the poor cannot hope to imitate, however cheaply. In the past a rich man's carpets could be matched by a poor man with a drugget or even with a cotton print, but today there is so great a variety of sofas, chairs, tables, cushions and curtains that a poor man cannot hope to attempt even a cheap imitation of them. In short, the distinctions between the rich and the poor have become wide and emphatic, and make for sharp contrast, resentment and bitterness.

The spread of knowledge, on the other hand, has made the common man more sensible of these differences and more sensitive to them. In the past, people used to adopt a more resigned attitude towards these matters. The common idea was that all wealth proceeded from God. If one was rich, it was because God had made him rich; and if the other was poor, it was because God had made him poor. This idea no longer holds. It is now felt that the poor are poor because they have been deprived of their share by the rich, and the rich are rich not because God has bestowed riches upon them, but because they have unjustly appropriated to themselves what really belongs to the poor. This change in the point of view has served to add to the resentment between the classes. In the past the poor man, if he was pious, was resigned and content. If he had to pass the time in hunger and privation, he accepted his lot as proceeding from God and praised the Lord accordingly, and if he found good and sufficient food for himself and his family, he praised the Lord for his beneficence. If a poor man was not so pious, even then he resigned himself to his poverty and helplessness and said nothing. Today, the responsibility, which used to be laid at the door of God, is fastened on the shoulders of man. It is felt that the rich oppress the poor, and this feeling adds to the bitterness between class and class.

At one time it was hoped that with progress in every direction, the disparities would disappear, but these hopes have not been realised. The advent of industrialism was viewed with apprehension by both sides. The rich said that the multiplication of machinery would provide large scale employment and ameliorate the lot of the workers. The workers feared that one machine would displace several men, and employment would be reduced. In spite of the increase of employment that has resulted from machinery, the distinction between the rich and the poor has become more emphatic than ever.

It is true that improvement has been effected in some respects here and there as the result of humanitarian effort by good-intentioned statesmen and industrialists, but these are only in the nature of alleviations, not an attack on the problem. The social systems have not been reformed, so the root of the evil remains.

Even today a rich man's dogs are fed on dainties left over from his table, while a poor man's children have to go to sleep on empty stomachs. This is no exaggerated contrast. There are hundreds of thousands of parents who have to put their children to sleep unfed. Even if the well-to-do were anxious to remedy this state of affairs, it would not be possible for them to achieve the desired end through individual effort. A rich man, however benevolent, cannot know that in a hut on a far away hill a poor man's child is dying of starvation? How can the opulent town-dwellers learn the vicissitudes through which the distressed populations of remote areas pass? True, often even the will to help is lacking, but assuming that the wealthier classes are willing and even anxious to help, they would lack the necessary knowledge and the necessary means by which they could banish poverty and distress from the world.

If a rich man feels out of sorts, his physician prescribes expensive patent medicines; and if the patient does not fancy the taste or smell of any of them, the same or another physician is ready to prescribe other equally expensive medicines. A rich man suffering from a common cold may spend on patent medicines what to a poor man may be a fortune. But when a poor woman's child contracts pneumonia she may beg in vain for a penny to buy the herbs for the brew which a country physician may have prescribed. The distress suffered by a mother's heart over her child's illness is the same whether the heart is that of a poor woman or rich, but the affluence of one enables her on the slightest occasion to command all the resources of medicine and pharmacy, and the penury of the other compels her to witness the severest sufferings of her child in abject misery. Does it not often happen all around you that the lives of the poor are put in jeopardy, or even lost, when only very little might have put them out of danger or saved them? The extremes of poverty which you witness all around often reach unendurable limits.

Once a poor woman came to me and took quite a long time to tell me the object of her visit. She said again and again that she had come to me with great hopes and appeared to be much afraid lest she should be disappointed. The more I tried to reassure her the more humbly she proceeded to entreat me. I imagined that she must be in need of money for the wedding of a son or daughter, but when at last I was able to persuade her to tell me what she needed, all she asked for was an eight *Annas*. I cannot forget the shock I experienced on that occasion. How long had she taken in coming to the point, how humble and hesitant had she been to put forward her demand, and how pitiful was the demand! Not more than eight *Annas*! It may be that she thought that nobody with means would be prepared to spare even eight *Annas* for a poor woman. Or, perhaps she imagined there were few who possessed or could spare an eight *Anna* coin for her. Whatever the reason of her fear and hesitation, it was a terrible extreme of misery which this incident disclosed. If she felt in common with all others of her class that nobody would be prepared to spare even eight *Annas* to afford relief to a poor woman in distress, then no wonder, the poor hate the rich so bitterly. If the poor, immersed in privation and misery, imagine that nobody has even eight *Annas* to spare, and the one who has is lucky, what a commentary would that be on the depth to which vast sections of mankind have fallen!

II

It was towards the close of the eighteenth century that reaction against this state of affairs began to take an organized form. The movement that was then started has been given the name of Democracy. It was recognized that the remedy lay not in the hands of individuals but in the hands of the State. As I have said an individual residing in Lahore or Delhi can hardly be expected to know that a poor woman's child is dying of starvation in a lone hut in the Himalayas. Nor would people in towns be generally aware of the conditions prevalent in the rural areas. But the State could be expected to possess, or should at least have the means of acquiring all this information. It was, therefore, thought that it was the duty of the State to undertake measures of relief and reform. As a corollary, it was urged that others besides the rulers, nobles and ministers should have a voice in the direction of a country's affairs, so that policies may be settled by the centre on the basis of the fullest information and knowledge. The first urge under Democracy was, therefore, to secure representation for different classes and interests, so that those in authority could be kept informed of conditions in different parts of the country and could have available to them advice from different sections. For some time these representatives exercised only advisory functions, but even that was a great step forward, inasmuch as it secured that those in power should have fuller information and knowledge concerning the needs and difficulties of those over whom they ruled.

At the outset these representatives belonged mostly to the landholding classes and the benefit of their advice, therefore, accrued principally to members of their own classes. Gradually merchants and manufacturers began to assert themselves, and the new movement known as Liberalism was started which charged itself principally with the safeguarding and promotion of the interests of these classes. As a consequence, the franchise was extended so as to cover these classes also, and they began to influence and even to direct the policies of the State.

Later on, another class began to struggle for recognition and for securing its rights. These were the workers in factories and offices, and when they perceived that only landed, commercial and industrial interests were represented in the legislature, they said that governments responsible to the legislatures so composed were not fully alive to their needs and sufferings, so they began to claim the right of direct representation for themselves. The policy and programme put forward on behalf of this class is known as Socialism. The principal object of this movement is to secure a more equitable distribution of wealth between the owners of capital and the working classes. For this purpose they are anxious to take the direction of government into their own hands, believing that this would result in a just redress of the grievances of the workers and other poor sections of the community.

The next stage came when it began to be felt that all these movements were national in scope and that their benefits were limited only to certain countries. It was said that improvement in the condition of workers in England, for instance, would afford poor satisfaction if workers in France continued to suffer privations and hardships. The remedy suggested was that workers in different countries should unite and co-operate with one another through international organizations and associations. Another incentive behind this movement was that it was believed that the capitalist classes were organizing themselves in active opposition to the working classes in different countries. It was felt that this could be successfully combated only by workers organizing themselves on an international basis. This movement is known as International Socialism.

The struggle for securing equitable treatment for workers and others received a great impetus and took on an entirely fresh orientation from the doctrines propounded by Karl Marx. This man was a German, Jew by race and Christian by faith. After anxious thought he arrived at the conclusion that the policy advocated by Socialism, that of persuading the capitalist classes by pressure was too slow and could not be expected to achieve the desired end within a reasonable length of time. He believed that it was futile to expect that those, who wielded political power, would be willing to reform themselves as the result merely of social or political pressure. He advocated that the only effective way of bringing about reform was for workers to seize power. Instead of carrying on agitation over a number of years for specific reforms and improvements, it would be far more effective for workers to take possession of the machinery of government and to carry out wholesale reform in the social, economic and political spheres. He, therefore, urged their direct participation in the political sphere with the object of seizing political power by means of which a complete social and economic revolution could be achieved.

Marxism is thus a development of International Socialism which aims at the achievement of its objects through political revolution rather than through economic change. It also points out that one reason for the failure of Socialism is that socialists believe in cooperation with the capitalist classes, whereas no real improvement can be hoped for without the overthrow of capitalists.

According to Marx, Democracy and all systems which base themselves upon the cooperation of the different classes proceed upon entirely erroneous principles. Under his system no quarter can be given to the capitalist classes and all power and authority must be appropriated by the workers.

For the achievement of this object he believed in violent revolution by organization and attack. It is this teaching of Marx which has taken practical shape in Bolshevism.

Marx was also of the view that the capitalist classes had been so long in power, and the workers had become so demoralised that the workers could not be expected to be able to safeguard their interests as soon as capitalists were driven out of power. You have heard the story of a poorly paid groom, who was urged by a friend to ask his master for a rise in pay and to leave the master if he refused to give him a rise. After considerable hesitation and much persuasion he made up his mind to act upon the advice. One morning when the master returned from his ride, the groom asked for permission to make a submission. On being told to go ahead, he blurted out "Sir, everybody in my position is getting much better pay than I am getting. I beg, therefore, that my pay should be raised, or." "Or, what, thou varlet?" thundered the master, administering a smart cut with his whip. "Or, I shall carry on as I am," whimpered the terrified groom. All his determination to secure a rise by threat of leaving his master evaporated as the result of just one stroke of the whip.

It is quite true that long suffering and privation deprive people of their stamina and will. I myself have tried to create some sort of ambition, some desire for improvement in the depressed classes. They will listen patiently but remark in the end with a somewhat superior smile, "God has ordered things as they are; it is no use trying to alter them." As if anybody who attempts to change or reform the existing order must be out of his mind. It is this attitude which led Karl Marx to observe that it was dangerous to vest workers and masses with direct authority in the beginning. According to him it was necessary to start with a dictatorship under which workers should be organized and educated and all class distinctions removed so that the next generation should grow up in an atmosphere of equality, and without any sense of inferiority. It is only then that political authority should be vested in the masses. Premature transfer of authority might put the whole movement in jeopardy.

Marx died, but no appreciable improvement followed. In fact, things became worse and worse. But here and there some men began to organize workers along the lines laid down by Marx. One of these was Lenin who subsequently became the first Dictator of Russia. Lenin and his colleagues gave definite shape to Marxian theories and carried on active propaganda among workers. They drew pointed attention to the contrast between the miserable conditions in which workers had to live and the luxury and extravagance which surrounded employers and their families. As their propaganda spread, it brought into existence several anti-Capitalist societies.

When worker organizations became strong enough, their leaders called together a meeting for the purpose of settling a line of action in the event of their coming into power. In the course of discussion at that meeting serious differences of opinion were disclosed between Lenin and Martof[*] who was also a powerful leader in the workers' movement. Lenin carried the majority with him and his party came to be known as Bolsheviks (that is the major party) and Martof's as Mensheviks (that is the minor party).

Lenin was a more orthodox follower of Marx than Martof. He believed that for the more effective

---

[*] In Russian at the end of a world v (Russian B) is written as v but pronounced as f. Here spellings are given accordingly.

achievement of their objects workers should not ally themselves with any other group or party. Martof, on the other hand, was of the view that until power was wrested they should work in cooperation with other active groups. In other words, Lenin put complete faith in the integrity of his own programme and policy and did not think it was necessary to rely on the help or cooperation of any other group or party to attain success.

Another difference between the two was that Martof advocated the establishment of a republican form of government from the very start, whereas Lenin held the view that dictatorship was inevitable during the first stages. It is possible Martof was influenced by the thought that if a dictator was chosen, Lenin would be the obvious choice.

Again, Martof insisted that under the new order, death penalty should be abolished from the start in accordance with the orthodox socialist principles. Against this, Lenin, while admitting the principle that the death penalty ought ultimately to be abolished, contended that it was not practicable to do so at the very outset. He urged, for instance, that it would be necessary to put the Czar to death after driving him out of power, for, so long as the Czar was alive, the Republic would be in danger. His hatred of the Czar was so deep that he was prepared to fight for the retention of the death penalty even though its only use was to put the Czar to death. As I have said, Lenin was able to carry a majority of the party with him, but when the revolution broke out and the Czar was compelled to abdicate, it was the Mensheviks who first came into power, as the other parties in the country were more ready and willing to lend them their support. This did not last very long, however, and the Bolsheviks were very soon able to assert themselves and to seize power.

III

I shall now proceed to describe the economic system advocated by the Bolsheviks. It must be remembered that the objective of this system is to stamp out the distinction between the rich and the poor and to see that everybody has food, clothing, and medical relief; and that all have their ordinary needs met according to a standard which should be the same for everybody. In short, their object is to do away with all the economic handicaps that operate against the poor. The principles upon which this system is based in accordance with Marxian theory are as follows:

(1) From each according to his capacity. For the sake of illustration, assume that one man owns ten acres of land and another a hundred. The levy from

each of them will not be equal or even in equal proportion. After allowing for the legitimate needs of each, the surplus will be taken away from him.

(2) To each according to his need. That is to say, in conjunction with the first principle whatever a person produces will be taken away from him subject to his being permitted to keep or to be supplied whatever he may stand in need of in accordance with a uniform standard. A man with less productivity but with a large family would yield less to the State and receive more from it in comparison with another with higher productivity and a smaller family.

(3) The surplus belongs to the State and must be employed for the benefit of the whole community, irrespective of whether the surplus is the result of labour or luck.

(4) That goods also, and not merely persons, should be subject to State control. That is to say the State should have the right to decide what shall be grown, and what not, in a particular locality. For instance, if a particular area is best suited for the cultivation of sugarcane, the State would direct that it should be devoted to the cultivation of sugarcane. Similarly, the growing of wheat or cotton may be prescribed for other areas. In other words, the State would prescribe in each case the use to which sources

of production would be put and everybody would be bound to obey.

(5) That intellectual effort divorced from manual labour has no value. The basis of all production is manual labour. Everybody must, therefore, make a contribution through manual labour, and those who refuse to do so shall have no claim upon the State or the community.

(6) To ensure the spread and successful working of these principles, a policy of offence rather than of defence should be adopted.

By the application of the first of these principles the Bolsheviks took possession of all property, wealth and other sources of production.

In accordance with the second principle, Bolshevism charges itself with providing for the needs of every manual worker. It is the duty of the Bolshevik Government to provide food, clothing, shelter, fuel etc., to each family in proportion to its numbers and also to make provision of medical attendance and relief. The only persons, who are excluded from the benefits of this system, are those who refuse to undertake manual labour and thus disentitle themselves to these benefits.

In accordance with the third principle, the State appropriates to itself all surplus in production and in the sources of production. For instance, if a peasant is able to produce 50 *maunds*[*] of grain on his holding, whereas his requirements could be met out of 20 *maunds*, the extra 30 *maunds* would be appropriated by the State. Or again, if a holding is in excess of the area sufficient to maintain the peasant and his family the excess area must be surrendered to the State.

As a result of the fourth principle, Bolshevism has deprived peasants, traders and artisans of all liberty of action by prescribing what each will or will not do. All agriculture, industry, trade and commerce must be carried on as prescribed by the State. The State determines what shall be grown or produced in each area and the peasants have no choice in the matter. The same is the case with other occupations and activities. Everybody has thus been reduced to the level of a task labourer.

The fifth principle has been utilized as a weapon against religion, inasmuch as by its application ministers of religion became disentitled to all relief. As a priest did no manual work, he was not entitled to have his needs fulfilled. The result was that the priestly class were compelled to devote the whole or the greater part of their time to manual labour, that is to say, to secular occupations.

A powerful attack on religion has been delivered

---

[*] maunds is an Indian Pakistani measure equal

by Bolshevism through adoption of the principle that religion should be a matter for the free choice of each adult. It is asserted that parents have no right to instil the principles of any religion into the minds of their children. Education and instruction should be wholly the concern of the State. It is alleged that to influence the mind of the child in the direction of a particular religion is tyranny of the worst type, as a result of which children grow up in the faiths of their parents. The proper course, it is asserted, is to safeguard the minds of children against all religious influence so that when a child grows into an adult, he or she can make a free choice in the matter of religion. The adoption of this view means the destruction of religion. Under it children are separated from their parents at an early age. Their education and instruction are placed in the hands of a State agency. All reference to religion or religious doctrines is excluded from the education prescribed. The result is that the child grows up completely indifferent to religion, if not actively hostile to it. It is no use asserting that when he arrives at the age of discretion he can adopt whatever religion he chooses. His mind, by that time, becomes completely sealed against every religious influence. It is claimed that the system ensures a clean slate so far as religious training is concerned, so that an adult on maturity is at liberty to write on it what he likes. This, however, is a patent fallacy. Under this system the child grows up in the belief that religion is nothing but a bundle of superstitions and by the time he becomes an adult, he becomes completely godless. The result is that the system ensures that future generations shall be confirmed atheists.

In accordance with the sixth principle, Bolsheviks began intensive propaganda to convert other countries. Their agents soon spread over the continent of Europe and in parts of Asia. In these countries they are known as "Communists." They have some sort of organization in the Punjab and other provinces of India also. Thus the principles preached by the German Jew, Karl Marx, obtained ascendancy throughout Russia, and the movement to secure the necessaries of life for every person, to abolish poverty and to establish equality between the rich and the poor began to have practical shape on a large scale. As the object of this movement was to bring about a universal revolution it produced certain reactions in other countries.

IV

The spread of Bolshevik doctrines in the continent of Europe was viewed by Italy and Germany with great apprehension. They had hoped to succeed to political and economic dominance in the world on the decline of the then dominant powers—England, France and the USA. Imagining that these older powers were entering upon a state of decline, these new powers began to cherish dreams of world dominance. Germany, Italy and Spain were in the forefront of those who fancied themselves in this role. To them the spread of Bolshevik doctrines seemed nothing less than the death-knell of their hopes and ambitions. Like vultures they hovered around a dying bullock. Germany and Italy were waiting for the collapse of England, France and the USA hoping they would succeed to a position of dominance and would be able to exploit the world for a long time to come. A movement, which had as its object the upsetting of all States as then conceived and organized, appeared to these new powers a very dangerous one and evoked a strong reaction in these countries. In Italy, it became Fascism under the leadership of Mussolini; in Germany, Hitler laid the foundations of Nazism; and in Spain, Franco became the leader of the Falangists.

All these movements were a challenge to Bolshevism which naturally made a strong appeal to the poorer sections in all countries. They imagined that under the Bolshevik system everybody would be supplied with an abundance of the necessaries of life—food, clothing, medicine; and that all their needs

New World Order

would be readily satisfied. Distance lends charm. So, in this country there are people who favour the Bolshevik system and believe that under that system the agents of the State go from house to house and deliver to the inmates food, clothing and such other articles as they may need. They do not realize that if this movement were to spread, the present economic system will go, and under the new one everybody would have food and clothing, but at the same time the surplus would be taken away by the State to be utilized by it in whatever manner it pleases.

People on the continent of Europe began to be affected by Bolshevik propaganda and began to lend their support to a system which promised to secure a comfortable living for everybody, and to do away all pain and privation.

As I have said, Hitler and Mussolini invented Nazism and Fascism as weapons to fight Bolshevism. They explained that under their systems, too, the State would assume control over industry and commerce and over the wealth of the nation and would bring about a more equitable distribution so as to afford relief to the poorer sections of the population. Under these systems the State became an intermediary between the man of capital and the worker, so as to secure better return and better conditions for the worker. On the other hand it was also stressed that it was necessary to foster the nation's resources and wealth by means of increased commerce and greater industrialisation, so that more wealth should become available for distribution among the poor. It was pointed out that for the promotion of national prosperity and the raising of the standard of living of the poor it was necessary to foster international commerce by means of which they could exploit other countries and utilize their wealth to relieve poverty and distress at home. For this purpose it was necessary to develop national shipping, national industry and national and international commerce. It was pointed out that big merchants and big industrialists helped increase national wealth and, like the goose that laid the golden egg, should be fed rather than starved. The greater the amount of wealth they produced, the more would it be available for distribution among the poor. It would be more beneficial for the workers and the poor that the industrial and commercial classes should continue to earn and accumulate wealth which could be continuously utilized for the benefit of the poor rather than that their wealth should be confiscated once for all.

It was next pointed out that Bolshevism was opposed to Imperialism and did not favour the domination of one people by another. On the other hand, England, France and the United States of

America had for a long time exploited other nations and countries through political or economic domination, and now it was their turn to enrich themselves by similar means. It was no use preaching to them that such a policy was open to objection for this reason or that. They were entitled to do what the other great powers had been doing hitherto. As it was claimed that this policy would relieve the poorer sections of their population, it naturally found favour with these sections.

It was further alleged that England, France and the USA were secretly encouraging the spread of Bolshevism, so that Germany and Italy should not be able to claim their legitimate share in the wealth of the world. This allegation also helped confirm the people of Germany and Italy in their opposition to Bolshevism.

Another aspect to which attention was drawn was that Germany and Italy were economically poor countries as compared with England, France and the USA. Even if the whole of their national wealth were distributed at once and equally amongst their people, no general prosperity would result, so that the enforcement of Bolshevik principles would not afford much relief to the poorer sections, nor make them as prosperous as the people of England, France and the USA were without Bolshevism. The introduction of

Bolshevism would prove fatal to these countries. On the other hand, the aggressive policy of Fascism and Nazism would result in the collapse of England, France and the USA and would enable Germany and Italy to appropriate the greater part of the wealth of the world, the distribution of which by the National Socialist State would set up a general level of prosperity much higher than could be achieved under the Bolshevik system.

These theories whether well or ill-founded began to attract support in Germany, Italy and Spain, in spite of the fact that Bolshevik propaganda had already had a start in these countries. The people of these countries began to hope that they would be more prosperous under the National Socialist system, than under the Bolshevik system. These countries, therefore, progressively adopted the National Socialist programme under different names with the object of pulling down England, France and the USA so as to be able to appropriate the wealth of these countries as well as of the rest of the world for their own use.

Another doctrine propagated by the National Socialists was that in order to strengthen their national system they had to fight not only Bolshevism but also such religious systems as received their direction and inspiration from outside. These systems were regarded as sources of strife and weakness. It was in pursuance of this theory that Hitler began to persecute the Jewish and Roman Catholic faiths. Afraid lest Jews, who occupied a position of predominance in Russia, should work for the spread of Bolshevism in Germany, Hitler adopted the policy of extermination of the race in Germany, even of those sections of it which had adopted the Christian religion. As the non-Catholic German people owe no spiritual allegiance to any authority outside Germany, he had no fear that they would at any time look for directions or guidance from any quarter outside Germany. He thinks that the Germans ought to have a distinctive faith of their own, however barbaric its doctrines may be. This theory has given rise to religious movements in Germany which seek to lead the German people to their pre-Christian pagan beliefs. One of these movements, for instance, which had the support of General Ludendorf and his wife, sought to restore the ancient worship of the dog in Germany. All this is the result of Hitler's view that no religion should be encouraged in Germany which has its centre outside the country. Italy has not adopted this doctrine to the same extent as Germany has. One reason for this is that Rome itself is the centre of the Roman Catholic faith. The Fascist Party, therefore, has not started any direct opposition to Roman Catholicism, but they have, to some extent, tried to check its influence, so that the Church should not interfere unduly with the political activities of the party. Later on, under Hitler's influence, the Fascists also began to adopt an anti-semitic policy, because it was pointed out to them that the Jews not only supported the Bolsheviks, but also tried to strengthen the three capitalist powers. Spain is opposed to Bolshevism and to the capitalist Powers but has not adopted any anti-semitic measures.

Hitler invented another doctrine to consolidate support for himself. He said that the theory of evolution had established that it was only the fittest who went forward and that the progress of the world depended upon the fittest being placed in a position of predominance. In accordance with this theory he contended that as the Aryan race had proved itself to be the best, it ought to occupy the position of the greatest predominance and that this applied more particularly to the Nordic Aryans, that is to say, the Germans. I cannot help observing that in this respect Hitler is a follower of Pandit Dayānand, for, it was Pandit Dayānanda who first advocated the theory of the superiority of the Aryan race. Be that as it may, Hitler urged that the right to rule others belonged to the Germans, they being the best part of the great Aryan race. He pointed out that even with regard to animals, people preferred to promote the best breed. And yet so far as the organization of the State was concerned, this principle was being ignored. He claimed that, as the Germans were the most superior race at the moment, they were entitled to rule over other races. He explained that this involved no injustice or unfairness. It was universally admitted that man should rule beast, not beast man. So should a superior race rule and exploit inferior races rather than be subservient to them. The Germans accepted this theory with enthusiasm.

V

There are, in short, three rival movements at present which have as their objective the relief of poverty and the removal of poverty and privation.

The first of these is Socialism which is gaining ground in the most powerful and advanced countries, the object of which is to admit the poorer sections to a gradually increasing share in power and to impose increasing State control over means of production. It also aims at raising the standard of life and the removal of want, by means of an increase in national wealth. This movement has been at work for some time in England, France and the USA, and there can be no doubt that it has brought about a certain amount of improvement and amelioration in the condition of the poor in those countries. A worker in these countries compares favourably with Government officials in this country who are supposed to be fairly well off. In our country an Extra Assistant Commissioner or a Sub-Judge is regarded as a respectable and a well-to-do official. The starting pay of such an official is about Rs. 250 a month, which is the equivalent of the average of a worker's wages in England. In the USA the standard is even higher. In that country, an ordinary worker earns the equivalent of between Rs. 500 and Rs. 700 a month. But he ranks only as a labourer. In short, those countries have not only striven to raise the standard of living but also to foster the sources of national wealth so as to secure an all round improvement in economic conditions. These benefits have been secured through the operation of Socialism as practised in those countries, but they are confined mainly to the people of those countries. No doubt the people seem very anxious to extend these benefits to other countries, but at the same time they are not willing to contemplate any diminution in the power and influence which they at present exercise over other countries. Take the case of India. A great deal of sympathy is professed and perhaps even felt for her, but all efforts to improve Indian conditions are circumscribed by the consideration that European interests in India should suffer no hardship. Their attitude towards India is like that of a kind master

NEW WORLD ORDER

towards domestic animals. He takes pleasure in feeding his stock well, but is careful that this should not be permitted to affect adversely his own standard of living. Similarly, when any concessions are proposed to be granted to India, care is taken that these should not affect prejudicially any Imperial interests. The British are naturally anxious that the standard of living of their own workers should not fall. For, in that case they would themselves fall to the level of countries like India or Afghanistan.

This movement suffers from two serious defects. In the first place, its sympathies are confined to the people of the respective countries which have adopted it. They are not universal. In other words, it is the secret ally of Imperialism, but professes sympathy with Internationalism, merely to make sure that other nations should not outstrip those which have put faith in the movement. The second defect, from which it suffers, is that the movement is purely secular and has no religious aspect whatever, so that even if the first defect is removed and the movement is made truly international, the religious side will remain completely neglected. This movement ignores the fact that spiritual needs require to be attended to even more urgently than purely physical needs. Those interested in the movement are not opposed to religion, but have no particular interest in it either.

That being so, they cannot be expected to make sacrifices for its sake.

VI

The second movement is one which is now being tried out in Russia. The cardinal points of this movement are that individual effort should be replaced by collective effort; that manual workers should be secured against want and privation; that purely intellectual workers should have no claim upon the State; that all surplus wealth should belong to and be at the disposal of the State; that the State should have full control and direction over the means and sources of production; that the education and training of children should be in the hands of the State and not of the parents; and that the movement should seek to gain universal acceptance. These people believe in the rule of the masses, but are not prepared to entrust political power to them for a considerable time to come. This movement is known as Bolshevism in Russia and as Communism in other countries.

It suffers from the following defects: its most serious defect is that it forbids individual effort. This perhaps is not realised fully at the moment, but its disadvantages are bound to be felt more and more as time passes. Man is so constituted that he is much more keenly interested in that which visibly promotes his own interest, or through him that of others but is not interested to the same degree in anything the benefit of which is not observed directly but seems rather remote. Our interest in our own work or occupation is stimulated by knowledge of the results we achieve. Under ordinary systems a student's interest in his studies is stimulated constantly by the urge towards the achievement of the objective he has set to himself. One may be working to secure respectable employment in the service of the State; another may desire to work up to the position of a Captain of industry; a third may wish to become a commercial magnate. In each case the motive may be to secure comfort for himself and those dependent upon him and to exercise power in a certain sphere. When this incentive is removed and the State determines that every person irrespective of his education or training and his intellectual capacity shall receive the same reward, intellectual effort is bound to decline and to be discounted. An average student will cease to put forth his best effort, and diligence will decline. There will be very few who will seek to pursue knowledge for the sake of knowledge; the majority will become comparatively indifferent. This attitude will spread to all occupations, professions, arts and sciences. The result will be a gradual decline in intellectual qualities.

Experience shows that intellectual qualities and acquirements are transmitted through heredity. That is why eminence in many arts and sciences is known to be inherent in certain families, tribes, races or nations. For instance, the Italians have always excelled as painters, sculptors and musicians. The Kashmiris are adepts at the culinary art and calligraphy. Other nations have attained eminence in other fields. Even among individuals, it is generally observed that the qualities of the father are repeated in the son and even remoter descendants. That moral and intellectual qualities are transmitted through heredity no longer admits of any doubt. It is true that environment exercises a very potent influence over an individual's development, but it is none the less true that an individual inherits many moral and intellectual qualities. Under the operation of the Bolshevik system the incentives towards high intellectual effort have been considerably weakened, and this is bound to result in the progressive deterioration of intellectual capacity.

The second defect in this movement is that it seeks to promote itself by force and violence, rather than by persuasion. If the movement had sought to bring about an equitable distribution of wealth by means of persuasion and conviction, results might have been wholly beneficial. It seeks to achieve this end, however, by force at one fell swoop. The wealthy sections have been deprived of all wealth and property at one stroke and have been suddenly plunged into poverty and misery. This kind of violent revolution is bound to lead to disaster. A change to be beneficial should be ushered in after conditions, suitable for it, have been provided. When a good gardener decides that transplantation has become necessary he carries it out after careful preparation and under the most favourable conditions. If this is not done, the plant is bound to wither and die rather than bring forth fruit. Bolshevism has paid no heed to this principle. The result has been that the old aristocratic classes had to go into exile and all their influence has been cast on the anti-Bolshevik side. They continue to do propaganda against Bolshevism in the countries of their adoption and to incite the governments of those countries against Russia.

Thirdly, by opposing religion the Bolsheviks have set the religious part of the world up against them. Those who are truly attached to religion will never be able to lend support to Bolshevism.

Fourthly, Bolshevism has opened the door to dictatorship. It is true that these people profess to believe in mass rule, but they say that dictatorship is necessary in the initial stage. We are not told, however, when dictatorship will come to an end. Lenin was succeeded by Stalin, and Stalin may be succeeded by Molotov and so on. Thus in practice this movement has resulted in setting up a rigid dictatorship.

Fifthly, this movement creates barriers in the way of intellectual development. Apart from the fact to which I have already adverted—that if all intellectual effort whether great or small is to have the same reward, very few will be impelled to high intellectual effort—this movement in effect imposes drastic restrictions upon intercourse between peoples of different countries and thus shuts down one of the main sources of intellectual stimulation. Providence has endowed different nations with different intellectual qualities. The Chinese mind excels in one thing, the Japanese in another, the French in a third and so on. History shows that it is only by free and unrestricted intercourse between nations that intellectual progress can be maintained at a high level. If foreign travel is permitted only to a few or can be afforded only by a limited number out of a nation, that nation will not be able to derive much benefit from the intellectual attainments of other nations, and as a result very useful technical and scientific knowledge will be lost. For instance, at one time the weavers of Dacca produced very fine muslin. Europe has since developed highly technical textile machinery which is capable of manufacturing cloth and fabrics of varied qualities, but they are still no match to the Dacca muslin. Similarly, the Egyptians possessed the secret of embalming and preserving the bodies of their dead in the form of mummies. I have myself seen some of these mummies in Egypt, and they are in a wonderful state of preservation. They are thousands of years old, and yet by looking at them one imagines they are bodies of persons who may have died but a few moments before. Even the freshness of their complexion is preserved. The world has made great progress in science and technology since the days of the ancient Egyptians, but neither in Europe, nor in America, nor in any other part of the world has anybody succeeded in discovering the process which the Egyptians employed for preserving the bodies of their illustrious dead. Modern methods of embalming the dead are a poor substitute. Again, it is related that in the Mughal palaces in Delhi there was a marble bath which could be heated with the help of a single lamp. When the British took Possession of Delhi, they took the mechanism to pieces in order to discover the secret of the heating arrangement, but having taken it to pieces they were not able to restore it. Different minds have different bents, and the reaction of one mind upon another is one of the main sources of intellectual stimulation which leads to development and progress. If one is with a farmer even for a very short time, one gathers interesting information and acquires new knowledge about agriculture; or, again, if one associates with a carpenter, one gains fresh knowledge with regard to his craft. Such contacts are not only stimulating but refreshing for the mind. If a Punjabi travels into the UP or into Kashmir, he is bound to return to his own province with increased knowledge of many things. That is why in the Holy Qur'an, God exhorts the Muslims to travel in different lands so as to increase their knowledge and to develop their minds and intellects. If a Muslim from India were to travel to Arabia by way of Iran and Iraq, he would increase his knowledge in many directions and his mind would become broadened and more richly equipped. If, however, everybody is to be given only that which would meet his ordinary needs, foreign travel would become very restricted, and as a consequence this valuable source of intellectual progress would run dry. It is essential for the intellectual progress of a nation that a section of it should devote itself to the study of the intellectual activities of other nations by personal association and by the observation of those activities on the spot so as to enrich the store of knowledge of their own people.

It may be said that agents of the State can undertake such journeys. But if this is to be confined to diplomatic and consular agents the object would not be served, inasmuch as it does not follow that those, who are trained in diplomacy or in the technique of commercial intercourse between nations, should possess minds adapted to the acquisition of scientific, technical and artistic knowledge. Where free intercourse is permitted, a doctor, a lawyer, an engineer, a painter, a sculptor, a poet or a religious leader, will gather information and knowledge suited to the pursuits and to the intellectual capacity of each, and the national intellect will be enriched proportionately in all these directions. If it is urged that the State could send abroad, at its own cost, representatives selected from various walks of life for this purpose, the answer would be that this would in itself result in setting up standards of discrimination and inequality which it is the declared object of the movement to abolish. It would merely prove that the doctrines of the movement were impracticable or inconsistent in at least this respect.

Sixthly, this movement promotes class struggle instead of putting an end to it, inasmuch as it involves the extermination of the rich and propertied classes.

Seventhly, when this movement begins to decline, its fall will be sudden and will lead to chaos. Other systems at least ensure a certain amount of continuity. Under a monarchical system one sovereign succeeds another. Under a system of parliamentary government there is a perpetual succession of parliaments. Bolshevism aims at securing a dead level in everything and does not encourage representative institutions. It also discounts purely speculative and intellectual activities. The result will be that when a decline sets in, the whole system will fall with a crash and will probably be replaced by absolutism as was the case with the French Revolution. It only produced an absolute Emperor like Napoleon and not a succession of great republican leaders.

VII

The third movement is National Socialism. This aims at raising the standard of the poor and yet preserving and encouraging individual talent and capacity. But as the leaders of the movement believe that the highest talent and capacity are monopolies of their own respective peoples, their object is to raise the German, Italian and Spanish people at the expense of other peoples and nations. The latest adherent of this movement is Japan. This movement is open to several objections:

It aims at the improvement of national standards at the expense of other nations and is not universal in its application.

Secondly, it too fails to provide for spiritual peace

and contentment and, on the contrary, imposes restrictions upon religion. The very idea of religion carries the notion that it is based upon divine injunctions; any limitations and restrictions put on it must also be imposed by divine command.

Thirdly, it exalts the individual unduly as against the collective wisdom of the nation. It may often happen that the views of one individual, however high his intellect, may be at fault compared with the collective views of a nation or a group, though the level of the collective intellect may not be as high as that of the individual. The system devised by Islam seeks to utilize in the service of the nation the individual as well as the collective intellect. It provides that the Khalīfah (Caliph), who himself is elected, should seek to guide himself by the advice of the representatives of the nation, but if he should, on any particular occasion, be of the opinion that in accepting and following the advice tendered to him he will be putting the national interest in jeopardy, he is entitled to overrule such advice. This system makes available to the nation at once the collective wisdom of the nation as well as the judgment of the highest intellect among them. But National Socialism carries the individual principle to an extreme. Have not all of you had experience of occasions when the whole village is in the wrong and one old man offers the best advice, or when the seniors may be in the wrong and the young men may be in the right?

All these movements possess certain extreme aspects which have led to friction and conflict between nations and the present war is the result of this conflict. The Bolsheviks desire that their theories should gain universal acceptance and their system should be adopted everywhere. The Socialist elements in England, France and the United States are anxious to safeguard the sources of wealth in their possession and have no desire to yield any of them to Germany, Italy or Spain. The first struggle that ensued was between the Socialists and the National Socialists. The Socialists wanted to retain their national wealth and power and the National Socialists desired to drain away that wealth and power into their own lands. Bolshevism was the last to enter the field. Eventually, Hitler was clever enough to come to some sort of understanding with Russia by offering her a bribe in the shape of a share in the loot in the event of the defeat of the Western powers. Russia pretended to be deceived by the offer and an agreement was patched up but after the collapse of France, when Hitler had succeeded in making himself master of greater part of Europe, he turned his attention towards Russia— impelled by various considerations the foremost of which was his need of oil, raw materials and other supplies. He had to postpone his invasion of Britain and was anxious to employ his powerful war machine for the achievement of some other objective. The only other objective he could think of was the destruction of Bolshevism. He, therefore, embarked upon an invasion of Russia, and thus brought about an alliance between Bolshevism and the Western Powers. Now two of these movements are on one side and the National Socialists are on the other. If the war ends in victory for the National Socialist powers, the poor of Germany, Italy and Spain will certainly stand to gain, but the rest of the world will be much worse off than before. That is to say, poverty may be relieved or even abolished in four countries, but will be intensified in all the others. On the other hand, if victory is won by the Allies, some countries may make an advance towards political liberty and some concessions may be granted to India, but so far as commercial and economic freedom is concerned, these countries will have to carry on a prolonged struggle for its achievement. For, not only will the old conservative and liberal parties stand in the way of this freedom, but even the Socialists will oppose it out of the apprehension that it might result in lowering their own standard of living. There can, however, be no doubt that other countries will be comparatively better off in the event of an allied victory than if the National Socialist countries are victorious.

So far as India is concerned, I have, on several occasions, expressed the opinion that in the event of a German victory, we shall be very much worse off and that a British victory is bound to lead to an improvement in India's affairs. Some of us are apt to imagine that if we are to remain a subject nation it is immaterial whether we are subordinate to this power or that, but this is an entirely mistaken point of view. I have already had occasion to point out that the older powers, having enjoyed economic domination over a long period, have now lost that aggressiveness characteristic of nations flushed with the acquisition of new power. These latter are likely to spring upon other nations like swarms of hungry locusts, whereas the older powers may now be compared to an old merchant, who has accumulated a large amount of wealth—he is miserly and acquisitive, but he may also remain content with things as they are. On occasion, he may even contemplate his possessions with satisfaction and may give up the desire to add to them. The older powers may be approaching a condition of surfeit, whereas those who are struggling to gain fresh power are certain to prove very greedy. Great Britain already enjoys dominion over the most tempting parts of the old world to the confines of China. The United States enjoys economic domination over the rest of the world. They are like a person who is already filled to repletion, and a person so well fed is not overmuch inclined towards high-handedness and tyranny. If you present such a person with a dish of *Pulā'u*[*], he will be inclined to partake sparingly of it, but if you were to place the same dish before a hungry person, he would not only clean it up but would probably demand your share of the meal also. The Germans, Italians and Spaniards are at the moment famishing. If they come to the top, they will achieve great feats of exploitation as the British did when they first began to dominate India. They will be inspired by similar desires and will subject other countries to ruthless exploitation for a century or two. The British, on the other hand, though they may still have the desire to exploit may wish to remain content with what they have already acquired, so that their desire for domination and exploitation is occasionally tempered with ideas of justice and fair play, and those who are subject to them are less liable to be subjected to tyranny and high-handedness.

Again, the older powers do not normally interfere in matters of religion and, except in extreme case or political or economic necessity, do not apply even secret or indirect pressure in these matters. Those, therefore, who have faith in God and in the value of Divine Revelation and believe that it is necessary for

---

[*] Indian dish of fried rice cooked with meat or vegetable curry.

the complete fulfilment of life here and Hereafter to act upon divine teachings, are bound vastly to prefer and desire the victory of the Western over the National Socialist powers, in spite of the fact that the attitude of the Western powers towards other nations is also somewhat selfish and leaves much to be desired.

We must not forget, however, that the victory of the Western powers necessarily means also the victory of Bolshevism, and Bolshevism is an even greater enemy of religion than the National Socialists. By the victory of the Allies, therefore, the world will be rescued from the dangers of National Socialism, but a new struggle will start between religion and irreligion.

VIII

I have so far dealt with purely secular movements. I now come to the schemes put forward by the followers of different religions for setting up a new order. Of these religions the principal ones are Hinduism, Judaism, Christianity and Islam. The followers of each of these faiths claim superiority for their particular faith, and allege that by following its teachings the world can get rid of all pain and tribulation. The Hindus proclaim that they will unfurl the banner of *Om* at Mecca (which God forbid). The

Jews assert that their law is superior to everything else. The Christians try to persuade that the teachings of Jesus alone are worthy of being practised. The Muslim claim, and rightly, that Islam alone prescribes efficacious remedies for the misery and suffering of mankind. I am not at the moment talking of the spiritual benefits to be derived from prayer and fasting. I am dealing with the question of want and poverty. I have referred to movements which have been started with the object of abolishing want and poverty. I now desire to discuss the theories which are advanced for the purpose by these great religions. In other words, what are the social and economic systems which these religions desire to see established in the world?

For this purpose I shall start with Judaism. The system advocated by Judaism is purely racial. There is nothing universal in it. For instance, Judaism teaches that the descendants of Israel alone are the chosen of God, and that the rest of mankind were created to serve them. If followers of the religion obtain a position of domination in the world, tyranny is bound to increase rather than decline. Again, Judaism forbids a Jew lending to another Jew on interest (Deut. 23: 19-20; Lev. 25: 35-37), but leaves him at liberty to lend on usury to others. Now, if the lending of money on interest is evil, why is this evil prohibited when the debtor is a Jew and permitted in the case of a Gentile debtor? The reason is that Judaism is a purely racial faith and permits in the case of Gentiles what it does not countenance in the case of Jews. If this faith were to prevail, it is obvious that it will impose levies upon Gentiles and distribute the proceeds thereof among the Jews. Similarly, Judaism encourages the spending of money for the relief of poverty and other charitable purposes, but restricts its application to the Jews alone. Under the Jewish Government, therefore, the benefit of all such expenditure will go to the Jews alone. Again, Judaism does not prohibit slavery, though it prohibits a Jew being made a slave permanently. That is to say, a Jew should not ordinarily be reduced to the position of a slave, but if he should happen to be one, this should only be temporary. This is secured by the ordinance that all Jewish slaves should be set at liberty every seventh year, (Deut. 15:12; Exod. 21: 2).

If a Jewish slave is purchased immediately after the expiry of one of these septennial cycles, he would be free after seven years. If he is purchased after the expiry of one year from the commencement of a new cycle, he will obtain his liberty after six years and so on (Lev. 25 : 39-46). That is to say, the maximum period during which a Jew can remain in slavery is seven years. The rest of mankind may be reduced to perpetual slavery, but with this Judaism has no concern.

Judaism also lays down very harsh conditions which must be imposed upon nations opposed to it.

"When thou comest nigh unto a city to fight against it, then proclaim peace unto it. And it shall be, if it make thee answer of peace, and open unto thee, then it shall be that all the people that is found therein shall be tributaries unto thee and they shall serve thee.

And if it will make no peace with thee, but will make war against thee, then thou shalt besiege it. And when the Lord thy God hath delivered it into thine hands, thou shalt smite every male thereof with the edge of the sword. But the women, and the little ones, and the cattle, and all that is in the city, even all the spoil thereof, shalt thou take unto thyself and thou shalt eat the spoil of thine enemies, which the Lord thy God hath given thee. Thus shalt thou do unto all the cities which are very far off from thee, which are not of the cities of these nations" (Deut. 20:10-15). This is with regard to foreign countries. With regard to the land of Canaan which was the promised land, the injunction is still more stringent. "But of the cities of these people which the Lord thy God doth give thee for an inheritance thou shalt save alive nothing that breatheth" (Deut. 20:16).

This is the social and economic system prescribed

by Judaism. If Judaism were to prevail, every male Gentile would be put to the sword and their women and children reduced to slavery. Not only Christian men, women and children resident in the land of Canaan but even horses, donkeys, dogs, cats, snakes, and lizards in the land must all be killed. For, the injunction is to kill everything that breathes. Under this system the Jews may obtain some relief, but other nations will be utterly destroyed.

The message of Christianity is that the Law is a curse. If the Law is a curse then all that it ordains or prohibits must also be a curse. Christianity no doubt preaches love, but Christian nations decline to act upon that teaching. If they had taken this teaching to heart, Europe should have presented a spectacle of perfect peace and not one of constant conflict and wars. Christianity—having declared the Law to be a curse cannot put forward any definite programme. For, whatever the programme, it will be a part of the Law and hence a curse. Its enforcement will bring no relief to mankind but will only increase their misery. Christian nations appear to believe that Divine Law, however, brief and simple, is a curse, but laws made by man, however complex, are blessings. The result is that for want of anything better, whatever a successful and dominant Christian nation strives after is described as the Christian ideal, whatever philosophy may at any time be in the ascendant is called Christian philosophy, and whichever social system becomes prevalent or popular is called the Christian system. If at any time Great Britain is predominant, it is the victory of Christian Socialism, if Germany comes to the fore it is also the victory of Christian Socialism and if the United States of America win the race for ascendancy, it equally is the triumph of Christian Socialism. Christianity is thus the ally of the successful and the victorious, so that whatever system becomes prevalent, it means the spread of Christian civilization. At one time, for instance, the prohibition of divorce was a characteristic of Christianity. Today divorce is dearly prized among the Protestant nations. Their faith is thus like a wax model which may be moulded into any desired shape; there is no danger of its breaking apart. Christianity as a religion, therefore, never had and never will have a programme.

The Hindu religion by inculcating the doctrines of *Karma* and transmigration of souls has completely barred the door of peace and progress upon mankind. Having a regard for these doctrines it is impossible to set up any new system designed to abolish the discrimination resulting from the unequal distribution of wealth. Once it is believed that a person is made poor as penalty for his actions in a previous life, nothing can be done to alter his circumstances in this life. One man may be born to a position of command

and domination as a reward for his actions in a previous life, another may be born into a state of poverty and misery as punishment for previous actions, and nobody has power to alter the circumstances of the one or the other. In the face of this doctrine the Hindu religion is not capable of putting forward a new programme for the progress of mankind. For, a new programme means an effort to bring about a change in the prevailing set of circumstances. But if the prevailing set of circumstances has been prescribed and ordained by the actions of mankind in a previous existence, it must be deemed to have been unalterably fixed and appointed, and nobody can have the power to alter it.

Another doctrine taught by Hinduism is that each section of mankind must act within a prescribed circle, and nobody has the power to go beyond it. The Brāhmins have their prescribed sphere of activity, and it is not open to a *Sudra* to take any of these duties upon himself. Nor is it open to a *Vaishya* to do what may be permitted to a *Sudra*, nor to a *Kshatriya* to act like a *Vaishya*. This doctrine also stands in the way of the abolition of discrimination between the rich and the poor. A system which has that as its object must equally safeguard the rights of all classes and must make adequate provision for everybody irrespective of caste. But against this *Manu* says, "No collection of wealth must be made by a *Sudra* even though he be able (to do it); for a *Sudra* who has acquired wealth, gives pain to Brāhmins (*Laws of Manu*, Tr. by G. Buhler, X, 129).

Under this law a Brāhmin or a *Vaishya* might collect millions, but if a *Sudra* should happen to save as much as five rupees to defray the expenses of his daughter's wedding it is the duty of the State to take away from him even this petty amount, merely because he is a *Sudra* and because a *Sudra* cannot save money. What scope is left here for any system which aims at improvement in the lot of the poor?

Again, it is written, "Even by (personal) labour shall the debtor make good (what he owes) to his creditor, if he be of the same caste or of a lower one; but a debtor of a higher caste shall pay it gradually (when he earns something)." (*Op. cit.*, VIII, 177). Operation of this law again would tend to keep a *Sudra* poor or to make him even poorer and to free a Brāhmin from obligations he may owe to *Sudra*. Far from affording any relief to the poor, it would tend only to add to their misery.

This doctrine of discrimination between the castes goes much farther. In the Case of the death of a person leaving behind him widows belonging to different castes, it is written: "Or let him who knows the law make ten shares of the whole estate, and justly distribute them according to the following rule: "The Brāhmin (son) shall take four shares, the son of the *Kshatriya* (wife) three, the son of the *Vaishya* shall have two parts, the son of the *Sudra* may take one share." (*Op. cit.*, IX, 152-153). Under this system what chance is there for a *Sudra* to improve his lot?

But this is not all. It is said, "A Brāhmin may confidently seize the goods of (his) *Sudra* (slave); for, as that (slave) can have no property, his master may take his possessions." (*Op. cit.*, VIII, 417).

This solves all the difficulties of the Brāhmins, for they are enjoined to take away whatever the *Sudras* may have collected and are even admonished to feel no qualms about it; for, this looting of the *Sudras* is no sin but an act of justice inasmuch as the wealth of the *Sudras* is not his, but belongs rightfully to the Brāhmins. This is the doctrine which the Hindu religion preaches, and inasmuch as, according to that religion, everybody except the Brāhmins and *Kshatriyas* and *Vaishyas* is a *Sudra*, that is to say, Syeds, Mughals, Pathāns, Pārsīs and Christians, etc., are all *Sudras*, the Brāhmins are rightfully entitled to dispossess all of them of whatever may ordinarily be supposed to belong to them and to appropriate it to their own use. If any of these should earn anything by his labour or by the exercise of his talents, and a Brāhmin should deprive him of it by force, he has no right of recourse to a court of law; for, if he should prefer a claim in a court of law, the judge would be bound to inform him that, according to the teachings of *Manu*, what he had earned was not his, but already belonged to the Brāhmin.

You must remember that I do not say that the doctrines taught by these religions today are the doctrines taught by the founders of these religions. It may be, a part of the original teachings of their founders was of temporary character and limited applications, and had served out its purpose long ago. On the other hand, a great deal of what is attributed to them today may not have been taught by them at all. Be that as it may, these doctrines cannot usher in an era of peace and contentment for mankind.

IX

I now come to Islam and proceed to explain the remedies suggested by Islam for the ills with which I have been dealing.

In the first place, Islam abolished the institution of slavery which had been established for thousands of years. I claim that of all the religions, Islam is the only one which abolished the institution by its own teachings, and that no other religion provides for its abolition. On the contrary, the institution was recognised in all other religions. In Judaism and Hinduism, slavery is a religious institution and cannot be abolished. Christianity is only a branch of Judaism, and slavery continued to be recognized among Christian nations for many centuries. When it was abolished, the abolition was brought about not by anything in the teachings of Christianity but by the progress which had been by then made in ethical standards. The history of the Church shows that efforts were made on many occasions to put an end to slavery but on each occasion the fiercest opposition was offered by the Church. In Hinduism, the caste system has established slavery so firmly and on so vast a scale that slavery in the ordinary sense becomes but a small evil by comparison. Islam abolished slavery altogether.

There is, however, one institution recognised by Islam which has been described as slavery and that is the taking of prisoners of war. But if this is an evil, it is a necessary consequence of war. When two nations are fighting each other, it cannot be expected that prisoners taken during the day would be set at liberty at night, so that they could return to their people and join the battle again on their own side the following morning. Even in certain games in which we are caught by the opposite side we have to be counted out for the rest of the game and are no longer at liberty to

NEW WORLD ORDER

participate in it for the rest of the innings. As a matter of fact, if prisoners could not be made during a war, or if it were obligatory to release them as soon as they were taken, wars would become almost interminable. This is, therefore, an evil which is a necessary accompaniment of war. Apart from this, Islam countenances no form of slavery. God says in the Holy Qur'an:

$$ مَا كَانَ لِنَبِيٍّ اَنْ يَّكُوْنَ لَهٗۤ اَسْرٰى حَتّٰى يُثْخِنَ فِى الْاَرْضِ ؕ تُرِيْدُوْنَ عَرَضَ الدُّنْيَا ۖ وَاللّٰهُ يُرِيْدُ الْاٰخِرَةَ ؕ وَاللّٰهُ عَزِيْزٌ حَكِيْمٌ ۝ $$

It is not for any prophet to have captives until he hath shed blood in war in the land. Ye desire the lure of this world and Allah desireth (for you) the Hereafter, and Allah is Mighty, Wise. (8:68).

It was not permitted to any prophet to make slaves of anybody. That is to say, not only was the Holy Prophet[sa] forbidden to make slaves but, according to this part of the verse, even previous prophets were not at liberty to do so, and, therefore, they did not actually do so. We must, therefore, conclude that neither Krishna nor Ram Chandra, Moses nor Jesus did so, and those who attribute this kind of conduct to them are not to be believed. The verse quoted above goes on to say that in the case of a war, which involves bloodshed on a large scale, it is permissible to take prisoners of war. This again indicates that prisoners of war may be taken only in wars between Nations or

States, but not of the result of tribal raids or family feuds. It then goes on to explain that those, who desire to enslave people or to make them prisoners under other conditions, are merely seeking worldly advantage and not the pleasure of God, whereas God desires that they should seek benefits for the life to come. God is Mighty, Wise: meaning that these injunctions like all God's Commandments are based on true wisdom, and that if they are contravened, and Muslims proceed to establish the institution of slavery, they will in turn be themselves enslaved. History tells us that among whichever people slavery became established, those people are reduced to the position of slaves. The Abbasides encouraged slavery and the result was that the majority of the later Caliphs were the issues of slave girls and though sovereign and free in name, in point of fact, they were no better than slaves. The word *Ithkhān* used in this verse for war means a war which is accompanied by bloodshed on a large scale and excludes the idea of tribal raids and frontier skirmishes. It presupposes a regular war between nations and organized states. A nation that does not desire to take the risk of any portion of the people becoming prisoners of war has only to avoid aggression. If it embarks upon aggression which leads to war and bloodshed, it cannot complain if some of its people become prisoners of war.

NEW WORLD ORDER

Islam, further, prohibits aggression, and the only kind of war permitted by Islam is a defensive war. In other words, it does not permit embarking upon war for the purpose, or in the hope of taking prisoners. The Holy Qur'an says:

أُذِنَ لِلَّذِينَ يُقَاتَلُونَ بِأَنَّهُمْ ظُلِمُوا ۚ وَإِنَّ اللَّهَ عَلَىٰ نَصْرِهِمْ لَقَدِيرٌ ۨ
الَّذِينَ أُخْرِجُوا مِنْ دِيَارِهِمْ بِغَيْرِ حَقٍّ إِلَّا أَنْ يَقُولُوا رَبُّنَا اللَّهُ ۚ وَلَوْلَا دَفْعُ اللَّهِ
النَّاسَ بَعْضَهُمْ بِبَعْضٍ لَّهُدِّمَتْ صَوَامِعُ وَبِيَعٌ وَصَلَوَاتٌ وَّمَسَاجِدُ
يُذْكَرُ فِيهَا اسْمُ اللَّهِ كَثِيرًا ۗ وَلَيَنْصُرَنَّ اللَّهُ مَنْ يَنْصُرُهُ ۗ إِنَّ اللَّهَ لَقَوِيٌّ عَزِيزٌ ۩
الَّذِينَ إِنْ مَكَّنَّاهُمْ فِي الْأَرْضِ أَقَامُوا الصَّلَوٰةَ وَآتَوُا الزَّكَوٰةَ وَأَمَرُوا
بِالْمَعْرُوفِ وَنَهَوْا عَنِ الْمُنْكَرِ ۗ وَلِلَّهِ عَاقِبَةُ الْأُمُورِ ۩

Permission to fight is given to those upon whom war is made—because they are oppressed, and most surely Allah is well able to assist them.

Those who have been expelled from their homes without a just cause except that they say: Our Lord is Allah. And but for Allah repelling some people by others, certainly cloisters would have been pulled down and churches and synagogues and mosques in which Allah's name is much remembered; and most surely Allah would help him who helps His cause; most surely Allah is Strong and Mighty.

Those who, should We establish them in the land, will keep up prayer and pay the Zakat and enjoin good and forbid evil; and Allah's is the end of affairs. (22:40-42)

That is to say, permission to go to war is accorded only to those who have been victims of tyranny and aggression, and this permission has been accorded because God wishes to demonstrate His power to help the oppressed against their oppressors. It often happens that aggression is embarked upon by the strong and powerful against the weak and helpless. In this verse God declares that Muslims have been permitted to take up arms in their own defence, inasmuch as they have been oppressed, and have been made the victims of aggression, and God has, therefore, determined to help them against their oppressors, so that those who are weak may overcome those who are strong. So that, not only was permission given to take up arms, but God declared that He would help and succour the oppressed to vanquish and overcome their oppressors.

The verse then goes on to say that Muslims were now permitted to fight inasmuch as they had been expelled from their homes for no other fault than that they had accepted Islam and had proclaimed Allah to be their Creator and Sustainer. It then says that a time would come when all war will be denounced as evil and appeals would be made in the name of humanity to put an end to it. The verse goes on to explain that it would always be necessary to check aggression by force. For, if that were not so, temples, monasteries, churches, synagogues and mosques dedicated to the worship of God, would all be destroyed. For, it is patent that the designs of an aggressor cannot be checked or frustrated merely because other people are anxious to live in peace and have no desire to go to war. One of the cardinal principles of Islam is to secure absolute freedom of faith, and the object of this portion of the verse is to explain that if war were absolutely prohibited, those, who desire to subordinate all matters of belief and religion to their own political authority, would be encouraged to embark upon aggressive and totalitarian policies and would seek not only to control political and secular activities but would endeavour to destroy religion altogether, and proceed to demolish places of worship. The verse then goes on to declare that God will help those who fight to secure freedom of religion, and that He being Strong and Mighty, those whom He succours will never be vanquished. It then goes on to state that people who are prepared to sacrifice their possessions and lives in order to secure freedom of faith, would not, if they come to power, exploit other people, but would worship God sincerely, distribute wealth equitably, eschew evil, put an end to the practice of evil by others and encourage the doing of good.

It is quite clear that a war of this kind can only be started by some aggressor against Muslims, and not by Muslims themselves. The responsibility, therefore, for prisoners being taken in such a war must lie on the shoulders of the aggressor who starts such a war. If he does not refrain from aggression and deliberately provokes war, he is certainly a menace and deserves to be made a prisoner. Such conduct is his own choice. If he had not sought to deprive others of spiritual freedom, his own liberty would not have been put in jeopardy.

Assuming that a war of this description becomes unavoidable and Muslims are forced to take up arms, the Qur'an enjoins:

فَإِذَا لَقِيتُمُ الَّذِينَ كَفَرُوا فَضَرْبَ الرِّقَابِ ۚ حَتَّىٰ إِذَا أَثْخَنْتُمُوهُمْ فَشُدُّوا الْوَثَاقَ ۚ فَإِمَّا مَنًّا بَعْدُ وَإِمَّا فِدَاءً حَتَّىٰ تَضَعَ الْحَرْبُ أَوْزَارَهَا

When you meet in battle those who disbelieve, then smite them until you have overcome them, then make them prisoners, and afterwards either set them free as a favour, or let them ransom themselves until the war terminates. (47:5)

That is to say, in a war so defined, you may take prisoners. But if you do so, you must adopt one of the two courses: When the war comes to an end, you must either release the prisoners out of pure benevolence; or, you must agree to release them on payment of ransom. If a prisoner is not released out of pure benevolence, he must remain in custody till he is ransomed, and during that period he must do suitable work for his captor. This cannot be regarded as hardship. For, even in modern times, prisoners of war are often put to such work as is suited to their capacity.

It appears to have been authorised by the Holy Prophet[sa] that a prisoner of war may be released on giving an assurance that he would not again take part in a war against Muslims. An incident which occurred in the time of the Holy Prophet[sa] illustrates this. In the battle of Badr, a prisoner was taken of the name of Abū 'Uzzah. The Holy Prophet[sa] released him on the promise that he would not participate in any subsequent war against Muslims. He broke this promise and fought against Muslims again in the battle of Uḥud. He was eventually again taken prisoner in the battle of Hamrā'ul Asad and executed.

To recapitulate, Islam prescribes two courses, one of which must be adopted in dealing with the prisoners of war. They must either be released without ransom or held in captivity till they are ransomed. While they are held in captivity, it is permissible to put them to suitable employment. But even with regard to this employment, Islam prescribes that no prisoner should be called upon to perform a task which is beyond his strength or capacity, and that he must be fed and clothed in the same manner as his captor. This is an injunction which goes far beyond the practice of modern States. Even those countries which are parties to international conventions are not under an obligation to feed and clothe prisoners of war on a scale and level which is prevalent in the case of their own citizens. This injunction was, however, very rigidly observed by the Companions of the Holy Prophet[sa]. On a particular journey, it is said, some of the Companions were accompanied by prisoners, and these prisoners themselves relate that the party ran short of provisions at a certain stage. The Companions, therefore, decided that they would feed the prisoners upon the remaining store of dates and would themselves subsist upon date-stones. It is related that there were not even enough stones to go round. It will be recognised that this injunction of Islam is very equitable and humane.

Another rule laid down by Islam is that no prisoner of war must be struck or beaten. If any prisoner of war is beaten or assaulted, he must be set at liberty at once. On one occasion the Holy Prophet[sa] on emerging from his house saw a Muslim beating a prisoner. This Muslim relates that while he was beating he heard the Holy Prophet[sa] call out:— "What are you about? Surely this is very un-Islamic. Do you not realise that God has much greater power over you than you have over this prisoner?" He said, he was terrified on hearing this and said, "O Prophet of God, I liberate him." 'The Holy Prophet said, "If you had not done so, you would have tasted the fire." These days many people have no qualms while beating their domestic servants, and yet the Holy Prophet[sa] called one of his Companions to account for beating a prisoner.

Another Companion relates that they were seven brothers and that they possessed a female prisoner, and on one occasion the youngest of them gave her a slap for some fault she had committed. When the Holy Prophet[sa] learnt of this, he said that the only penalty for the slap was that she must be liberated, and this was done. In other words, it was not only serious beating or striking that was prohibited, but even a slap involved liberation, inasmuch as such conduct indicated that the person guilty of it was not fit to be entrusted with the custody of, or authority over, another human being.

The Holy Qur'an also prescribes that marriage should be arranged for such of the prisoners as have arrived at, at the age of matrimony:

وَأَنْكِحُوا الْأَيَامٰى مِنْكُمْ وَالصّٰلِحِيْنَ مِنْ عِبَادِكُمْ وَإِمَآئِكُمْ

Marry those among you who are single and those who are fit among your male prisoners and your female prisoners. (24:33).

Could humane consideration go any further? Islam says, 'Feed them with the food that you eat; give them to wear the kind of clothes you wear; subject them to no kind of hardship; make arrangements for their marriage; and if ever any of you should happen to strike any of them the only penalty for this is liberation.' Many of them may be released unconditionally or only on condition that they will not again participate in a war against Muslims. I doubt very much whether today the most civilized State would forego reparations merely on condition that prisoners of war released by it shall not again participate in a war against itself.

It is necessary to say a word here in explanation of the system of ransoming prisoners of war. As I have already said, the first injunction of Islam is to release prisoners of war without ransom, but if a captor cannot afford to do this, he must release his prisoner or prisoners on receipt of ransom which is only a sort of reparation, or a recoupment of the expenses incurred by the captor on account of the war. The difference between conditions then prevailing and those prevailing today is that in those times each warrior had to provide his own arms and equipment, and reparation was also exacted by individuals. There were no regular armies nor any arrangements for the maintenance or custody of prisoners of war on a large scale. Prisoners of war were, therefore, distributed among those who had borne the expense of the campaign and had made sacrifices in respect of it. Now that modern States maintain regular armies, and in times of war all military activity is financed and provided for by the State, reparations are also a matter of settlement between the belligerent States, and arrangements for the maintenance and custody of prisoners of war are also a state responsibility. On the conclusion of peace all questions of reparations, penalties, exchange and release of prisoners have to be settled between the belligerent States. Reverting, however, to the Islamic teachings in this connection, what I desire to stress is that a prisoner of war could always secure his release by the payment of ransom. This payment could be made by himself or by his relatives or by the tribe of which he was a member or by the State of which he was a subject. There is nothing in these regulations which imported perpetual loss of liberty.

It may be argued that a prisoner may himself be poor and unable to pay his ransom. His tribe or state may be indifferent. His relatives may be hostile to him and may desire the prolongation of his captivity and his captor may be poor and so burdened with the expense which he had been compelled to incur on account of war, that he may not be able to afford his release without ransom. Then what chance is left for the prisoner to obtain his release? Even this contingency is provided for in Islam. The Holy Qur'an says:

وَالَّذِيْنَ يَبْتَغُوْنَ الْكِتٰبَ مِمَّا مَلَكَتْ اَيْمَانُكُمْ فَكَاتِبُوْهُمْ اِنْ عَلِمْتُمْ فِيْهِمْ خَيْرًا ۖ وَّاٰتُوْهُمْ مِّنْ مَّالِ اللّٰهِ الَّذِيْٓ اٰتٰىكُمْ ۗ

And those who ask for a writing from among your prisoners, give them the writing they desire, if you find that they have the capacity for it, and give them of what God has given to you. (24 : 34).

That is to say, "If any of your prisoners should be unable to provide for their ransom but should be willing to purchase their liberty on condition of paying their ransom by instalments, you should settle instalments with them and give them a writing in respect of it, if you think that they possess enough capacity to discharge the instalments out of their earnings. If in such a case you can afford to lend them money by way of capital for their ventures you are enjoined to do so." From the moment such a writing is given, the prisoner is free to dispose of himself in any manner he likes and is competent to hold and dispose of property and subject only to the obligation of the due discharge of instalments.

A captor has no right to refuse a prisoner liberty on the basis of instalments, unless the apprehension of war still continues, or the prisoner is an idiot or is otherwise unable to earn on his own account, and it is feared that if he is left to himself he is likely to do himself more harm than good. It may be objected that a captor might take unfair advantage of this exception and seek to continue a prisoner in bondage on the pretext that he is deficient in intelligence. But the Islamic law provides that a prisoner is always at liberty to apply to a magistrate for a settlement of instalments in case instalments are refused by his captor, or in case the settlement offered is unfair.

If, in spite of all these facilities, a prisoner of war fails to take advantage of them, it can only mean that he prefers the condition in which he is to the condition to which he might be restored in case he is set at liberty. The truth is that many of those who were prisoners in the custody of the Companions of the Holy Prophet[sa] did prefer to continue in that state rather than seek to revert to their original condition of nominal liberty. They were treated by their captors as equal members of their own families and found themselves very much better off than they had been as free men. The Companions provided food and clothing for them as they provided for themselves, set them no tasks beyond their strength, did not ask them to do anything in which they were not prepared to participate themselves; subjected them to no ill-treatment and were very ready to liberate them on payment of ransom in a lump sum or by instalments. It is true that these prisoners were technically held in bondage but often the light of Islam penetrated into their hearts, and they, had no desire to revert to their original condition. This is well illustrated by the case of Zaid^(ra) Bin Ḥārith^(ra) who was at one time a slave of Ḥaḍrat Khadījah^(ra).

Zaid^(ra) was not a slave in the ordinary sense but belonged to a free Arab family. He was taken prisoner in some local raid and came eventually into the ownership of Ḥaḍrat Khadījah^(ra). When the Holy Prophet^(sa) married Ḥaḍrat Khadījah^(ra), (though this was long before the commencement of his ministry), she placed all her property and belongings including Zaid^(ra) at his disposal. The Holy Prophet^(sa) gave Zaid^(ra) his liberty, but he continued to reside with his master. Eventually, his father and uncle discovered his whereabouts and came to the Holy Prophet^(sa) and begged him to let Zaid^(ra) go back with them. The Holy Prophet^(sa) told them that he had already set Zaid^(ra) at liberty, and that he was free to go wherever he liked. They then tried to persuade Zaid^(ra) to accompany them back home, but he refused saying that though he had been set at liberty, he had no desire to forsake the Holy Prophet^(sa) and was determined to continue in his service. His father and uncle pleaded long and hard with him and told him that his mother was suffering dreadful pangs on account of separation from him, but all this failed to move Zaid^(ra), who reiterated that he could not expect his parents to treat him with kindness and affection greater than he received from the Holy Prophet^(sa). Surely nobody could have any objection to bondage of this kind, if in truth it was bondage at all.

NEW WORLD ORDER

One is surprised that such a bond of affection and kindness should have existed between two human beings, between whom the technical relationship was that of master and slave.

If in early Islam, therefore, some people preferred to remain in bondage rather than claim their freedom, it was by their own free choice. They realized that they were much better off in bondage than if they were free. But European missionaries continue to proclaim vociferously that Islam carried on the institution of slavery. Your attendance here is an illustration of what I have in mind. Is it not our experience that in ordinary meetings if even the most eminent lecturer exceeds his time by a few minutes, the audience begins to exhibit its impatience in many ways. Here so many thousands of you sit in great discomfort for hours together, cold and hungry, listening to me and wishing all the time that I should go on speaking. What is this difference due to? Is it not due to your having believed in the Promised Messiah[as] and having surrendered your hearts to his bondage? Is this kind of bondage open to any objection? Is it not rather an indication and a measure of true faith? It is to be bound not to man but to God.

In short, it cannot be urged that slavery was abolished by advance in civilization. Slavery was abolished by Islam. True, in Islam it was permitted to take prisoners of war, but even with regard to them, rules were framed which were in advance of those which the Allies and the Axis Powers observe today. Let me briefly recapitulate them. Prisoners could only be made in a war waged to secure freedom of religion. At the end of the war they must be released either without ransom or on payment of ransom. Ransom may be paid by the prisoner himself, or on his behalf by his relatives, tribe or State. If this cannot be arranged, the prisoner can ask for settlement of instalments and on these being settled, he is free to labour and earn as he may choose.

So much with regard to slavery or quasi-slavery. I now turn to the slavery which in practice results from economic conditions. Before I go on to explain the remedies which Islam has proposed in this field, it is necessary to remind ourselves of the theories which lead to that discrimination between the rich and the poor which we observe today.

First, it is sometimes said that as in the last resort most people act upon the rule of might being right, the rest of mankind is forced in sheer self-defence to follow it. For instance, the British when they possessed the power took whatever they could lay their hands on. Other countries may, therefore, consider it quite legitimate to follow in their footsteps. Thus when Italy invaded Abyssinia, Mussolini was at

NEW WORLD ORDER 75

pains to explain that the object of the invasion was similar to the object with which the British had made themselves masters of India: to extend culture and civilization. He said that the British claim was that they were holding on to India as they were anxious to bring it upto the level of other advanced and civilized countries. Mussolini claimed that his countrymen were in no sense behind the British in their anxiety to help and serve backward countries, and that his attack on Abyssinia was inspired wholly by these motives.

Secondly, some people contend that the State ought not to attempt any control in the economic field and that things should be left to adjust themselves by actual working. These people believe that the able and the strong are entitled to forge ahead and should not be subjected to any artificial control.

Another theory is that race differences are a reality which cannot be overlooked and that the due allowance must be made for them. The Hindu caste system is based upon and justified by an appeal to this theory. Under this system caste is determined by birth and the discrimination that results therefrom cannot be modified or abolished.

A fourth theory is pithily expressed in the saying "Majority has authority." In pursuance of this theory a minority is not entitled to any voice in the affairs of a nation and is often ruthlessly suppressed.

Another theory is that, that which has no owner belongs to the first finder. This doctrine was very familiar to us as children. Whenever any of us found something lying about in a manner which indicated that it had either been lost or thrown away, we would appropriate it by repeating the formula, "He who finds keeps;" as if that justified all such appropriations. But the articles to which children apply this formula are generally of no value. The Holy Prophet[sa] was asked what was to be done with an ownerless article. He asked the questioner to explain what he meant. The questioner asked what was he to do if he came across a stray goat in the desert? The Holy Prophet said, "In that case you must call out for its owner, and if in spite of calling out for him you are unable to find him, you may appropriate the goat, for, if you will not do that, it will be devoured by a wolf". He was then asked what was to be done with a stray camel. He replied, "You have no concern with a stray camel; it can feed itself and look after itself, you should set it at liberty." The questioner then said: "What am I to do, O Prophet of God, If I find a bag of money?" The Holy Prophet replied, "If you find a bag of money, take it up and continue to proclaim the fact till its owner appears and then restore it to him." So, there is a different rule for different articles. If the article found is certain to be destroyed, it may be

New World Order

appropriated after a reasonable effort has been made to find the owner. If it is liable to no such danger, it should be left alone. If it is in danger of being lost but can be preserved without much trouble or inconvenience, it should be so preserved, and efforts be made to find the owner, and when the owner appears it should be restored to him. In great contrast with these Islamic principles is the theory which European nations have followed in respect of weak and helpless peoples. They think that they are entitled to appropriate whatever is without an owner or whatever belongs to a weak nation. Australia is a great continent, but it has been appropriated by the British as an ownerless tract of land. India is a vast country with a huge population. This also has been appropriated by them on the same principle. The same applies to other European nations who have possessed themselves of vast continents like North and South America and groups of Islands; the principle being that a newly discovered country or continent, or a country having a weak government belongs to the first comer.

In addition to these theories there are some practical defects, and shortcomings which intensify the discrimination between the rich and the poor and the privations suffered by the poor. The first of these is that in the past the State has not charged itself with the responsibility for the needy and the helpless. In more recent times some Governments have begun to pay, attention to this matter and departments have been set up which are charged with the responsibility of providing relief. But these schemes of relief even now fall short of that which Islam has devised. Secondly, institutions the operation of which tended to draw wealth into the hands of a limited section of people have been permitted to flourish unchecked. Thirdly, doctrines have been allowed full play which serve to tie up wealth in hands in which has been permitted to accumulate. Fourthly, large portions of national wealth have been allowed to be spent on non-beneficial pursuits and objects which have been given the name of Art.

Islam has put a check on all these evils and has opened the door of progress for all mankind. It has set about achieving this object in the following manner:

First, Islam teaches that whatever Providence has created is for the benefit of all mankind and not for any section of it, though it may be that on the surface it looks as if some goods are assigned or committed to the care of a particular people. This is the same as a mother sometimes hands over a plate of sweets to one child who is told to share it with all his brothers and sisters. In the same way God says in the Holy Qur'an:

هُوَ الَّذِىْ خَلَقَ لَكُمْ مَّا فِى الْأَرْضِ جَمِيْعًا

That is to say: "Whatever there is in the earth has been created for all of you." (2:30)

By inculcating this principle Islam has rejected Imperialism, National Socialism and International Socialism: for, all these systems contemplate domination of powerful, technically equipped and well-organised nations, over weaker nations. We observe the tendency to this in several forms and directions even today. Apprehensions have been expressed that if the independence of India were to be recognised, it might result in the African tribes putting forward claims for their own freedom and independence, whereas they were and still are in a very low state of culture. At the time of the advent of the European nations into the Dark Continent, the African tribes used to go about naked and used to subsist upon whatever nature out of her abundance had provided. The Europeans introduced the rudiments of culture and civilized existence among them. It is claimed that that somehow gave the European nations a sort of right of proprietorship over Africa, and in any case entitled them to a position of dominance in that continent. Islam recognises no such right. No nation has been entrusted with the mission of civilizing other nations or of forcing any particular sort of culture upon them. The Qur'an lays down that whatever God has created is for the benefit of the whole of mankind (2:30). Islam has negatived the claim of any nation to a monopoly of any kind. Islam does not support any doctrine whereby South Africa could be reserved exclusively for the Boers and the British, or whereby the continent of America could be reserved exclusively for a few nations and all the rest of mankind could be shut out from sharing the benefits provided by the natural resources of these countries.

Similarly, Islam seeks to reduce the power and influence of those who are engaged in the production of wealth by harnessing or utilizing natural resources and who then claim complete control over the wealth so produced. Islam says that the community at large is also entitled to share such wealth, inasmuch as natural resources which have been created for the benefit of the whole of mankind have been used in the production of this wealth. For instance, all mineral wealth belongs to the nation or to the community, and no particular individual is entitled to its complete appropriation. Islam prescribes that 20% of all mineral wealth that may be exploited must be paid to the State to be utilized for the benefit of the community at large. This is in addition to the liability to pay Zakat to which all accumulated wealth and capital are subject under the Islamic law. By this provision with regard to mineral resources the State becomes part-owner of these resources, and on their being exploited receives 1/5th of the profits for the benefit of the community at large. This provision serves as a corrective to the evils that might result from uncontrolled exploitation of these resources.

Again, Islam teaches:

لَا تَمُدَّنَّ عَيْنَيْكَ إِلَىٰ مَا مَتَّعْنَا بِهِ أَزْوَاجًا مِّنْهُمْ وَلَا تَحْزَنْ عَلَيْهِمْ وَاخْفِضْ جَنَاحَكَ لِلْمُؤْمِنِينَ ۝

Do not look with longing eyes at that which belongs to other people, even for the purpose of taking care of it on their behalf grieve not over the condition of other people, but employ yourselves in the betterment of your own. (15:89)

The whole of the modern system of colonization is based upon the vicious claim that one nation is entitled to seize upon the lands of another for the purpose of introducing improvements in that country. Not only is this alleged principle false and untenable in itself, but its hollowness is soon demonstrated in practice; for, the dominant nation in practice does not even pretend to share the exploited wealth of subject countries with their peoples. Take East Africa, for instance. A comparison of wealth and prosperity of the European settlers with the poverty and destitution of the original inhabitants of the country would show beyond doubt how this principle operates in actual practice. Islam, therefore, teaches that each people should concentrate upon improvements in its own conditions and circumstances and that no people under any pretext whatsoever should exploit another.

It may be objected that this might put an end to all cooperation between different sections of mankind. This is not so. Islam does not forbid cooperation between one nation and another for mutual improvement or by way of service. It forbids political or commercial domination. A professor or teacher serves by offering his talent in return for adequate reward, but no nation is willing to serve another on this basis. The fashion today is to assume control over the people and resources of another country, with the result that the people of the country itself are deprived of the main benefits of those resources. Islam forbids this, and declares it unlawful for one people to assume political domination over another. Mankind are free to associate, but it must be by way of service and cooperation. The Bolsheviks in theory disclaim all intention of dominating other people but in practice they too subjugate non-Russian nations. Their attack on Finland is an example. The colonial problem which presents so many difficulties can be satisfactorily solved only along Islamic lines. All other solutions are ineffective and are, in fact, devices only for prolonging the system.

X

A third principle that Islam teaches is that so long as the nations of the earth are not ready to federate in a World State, a system of international security should be established along certain practical lines. The Holy Qur'an says:

وَاِنْ طَآئِفَتٰنِ مِنَ الْمُؤْمِنِيْنَ اقْتَتَلُوْا فَاَصْلِحُوْا بَيْنَهُمَا ۚ فَاِنْۢ بَغَتْ اِحْدٰىهُمَا عَلَى الْاُخْرٰى فَقَاتِلُوا الَّتِىْ تَبْغِىْ حَتّٰى تَفِىْۤءَ اِلٰۤى اَمْرِ اللّٰهِ ۚ فَاِنْ فَآءَتْ فَاَصْلِحُوْا بَيْنَهُمَا بِالْعَدْلِ وَاَقْسِطُوْا ۗ اِنَّ اللّٰهَ يُحِبُّ الْمُقْسِطِيْنَ ۝

And if two parties of believers fall to fighting, then make peace between them, and if one party of them transgress against the other, fight ye that which transgresses till it returns to the command of Allah; then, if it returns, make peace between them justly, and act equitably. Lo! Allah loveth the equitable.

(49:10).

That is to say, if two or more States should go to war with each other, it is the duty of the rest to try to bring about a settlement between them, but if this effort should fail and one of them should commit aggression against other or others, then all the rest should combine to resist the aggressor. When the aggressor has been defeated, the original dispute should be settled by the other States on an equitable basis. There should be no attempt to impose penalties upon the aggressor as a punishment for starting hostilities, nor should there be any attempt on the part of the intervening States to seek benefits for themselves. The settlement should be confined to the original dispute.

This verse is really in the nature of a prophecy. At the time when this verse was revealed, there were no Muslim parties which were likely to go to war with each other. The verse only makes provision for the future. The words fighting and transgressing indicate clearly that the principles laid down in this verse have reference to States. The principles which it lays down are as follows:

(1) If two or more States should fall out among each other, the other states should intervene and try to compel the States between whom a dispute has arisen to submit their dispute to arbitration.

(2) If any of them should embark upon aggression, all the others should combine to resist the aggressor.

(3) When the aggressor is defeated, all the States should settle the terms of peace, and in this settlement there should be no element of revenge or punishment.

(4) The matter in dispute is to be settled equitably. It may be that the aggressor State was actually in the right. The mere fact of aggression should not operate to deprive it of its right.

(5) The word 'equitably' indicates that the intervening States should not seek any benefit for

themselves at the expense of the victor or the vanquished.

This system of international security was laid down at a time when nobody had even started thinking about these matters. The significance of this verse was revealed to me, and nobody will deny that the true exposition of a text prescribing the limits of a system so vital to the security and prosperity of mankind is the function only of prophets and their spiritual successors. These principles affect the security of the whole of mankind and will continue to be utilized through centuries till the different nations of the earth are able to participate in the setting up of an International World Federation. I explained these principles in my book, *Ahmadiyyat or the True Islam*, published in 1924, and sounded a note of warning that unless the League of Nations was organised along the lines here indicated, it would fail in its main purpose, and unfortunately that has proved to be the case.

When I went to England in 1924 to participate in a Conference of Religions, the League of Nations had only recently been organised. Russia and Germany were then anxious to become members of the League. I pointed out the defects from which the League suffered in the light of the very principles to which I have just made reference. I made it quite clear that unless these five principles were kept in view the

League was bound to fail. I then stated:

"If these defects are removed, a League of Nations could be constituted in accordance with the principles laid down in the Holy Qur'an. It is only such a League which can do any good, not a League which for its very existence is dependent upon the courtesy of different nations." *(Op. cit. p. 337)*

Again, I said:

"So long as people do not realise in accordance with the Islamic teachings that all mankind are one people, and that all nations are subject to the law of rise and fall, and that no nation has continued always in one condition, it will be impossible to establish peace. We must remember that the volcanic forces which raise and bring down nations have not ceased to operate. Nature continues to be active as it has been through the centuries. A nation that treats another nation with contempt initiates an unending circle of tyranny and oppression". *(Op. cit p 360)*

People at that time seemed very pleased and proud about the League of Nations. I insisted that peace could not be secured unless all States were under an obligation to go to war with an aggressor, but this was not an acceptable proposition at the time. It was pointed out that any obligatory undertaking of this kind would lay the foundations of war rather than of peace. Not only this principle, but all the other Islamic principles that I have today expounded have been opposed during this period by all the new movements that have been started as bases of a New World Order. But after the unfortunate experience of the last twenty years, nations are beginning to turn in the direction indicated by Islam. Many people are beginning to advocate that under the security system to be established after the war there should be a compulsory obligation to oppose an aggressor by force. Even now I declare that if this security system is not based on Islamic principles it will end in failure.

XI

The principles I have just explained are designed to secure international peace. In the absence of international peace, it is not possible to secure conditions of national progress. But even after peace has been secured, it is necessary to carry out improvements in national conditions. I will, therefore, now turn to the means adopted by Islam for securing improvements.

With this object in view Islam has put forward four principles every one of which is designed to secure a more equitable distribution of wealth. One of the principal causes of social inequality is the accumulation of property and wealth in a few hands, so that the common people are deprived of all chances of acquiring property for themselves. To deal with this evil Islam compulsorily distributes property among a large number of heirs. On the death of a Muslim, his parents, widow, sons and daughters, all succeed to their shares in the property left by the deceased. Nobody is at liberty to modify in any manner the share to which each heir is entitled under this system. The Qur'an says that any attempt to interfere with this system is sinful. As compared with the Islamic system of inheritance, other systems suffer from various defects. Under some of them landed property is inherited by the eldest son alone, and under others females are excluded from inheritance by males. Manu, for instance, has laid down that daughters shall be excluded in the matter of inheritance by sons. Under all these systems property is confined in the hands of a comparatively small section of the community and the poor sections are deprived of all chances of improvement in their economic condition. As against this, Islam teaches that unless property and wealth are widely distributed, the community as a whole will not be able to progress. Under the Islamic system if a man has succeeded in accumulating property worth a lakh of rupees, it will be divided on his death among all his children, his parents (if still alive) and his widow if she survives him. In the course of a couple of generations, the original patrimony will have been so divided and subdivided that everyone of the numerous heirs of the original propositus will be compelled to exert himself to earn a respectable living instead of wasting his talents and living comfortably with the help only of inherited wealth.

Secondly, Islam forbids the hoarding of money, that is to say, it directs that money should be constantly in circulation. It must either be spent or invested so that it constantly fulfils its primary object as a means of exchange, and should promote commercial and industrial activity. A contravention of this direction is regarded by Islam as entailing grave divine displeasure resulting in dire penalties. There is a verse in the Qur'an which says that those who accumulate gold and silver in this life will be punished by means of the same in the life to come. The significance of this is obvious. If people were at liberty to accumulate money and precious metals which are the equivalent of currency, so much wealth would be withdrawn from circulation and, as a result, the community at large would be so much the poorer. If money is put constantly back into circulation, it helps to promote beneficent activities of all kinds, and thus serves to relieve poverty and distress by providing employment and stimulating effort. Take a simple illustration. If a person having a certain amount of money decides to build a residence for himself, or so construct a building for a public purpose, then, apart from the achievement of his object, he will by this means have provided employment for a number of brick-layers, masons, carpenters, iron-smiths, and so on. This would not have been the case had he merely kept the money locked up in his house or in a bank. Even in the case of Muslim women, although Islam permits them to wear ornaments, it discourages the expenditure of large amounts of money for this purpose.

Thirdly, Islam forbids the lending of money on interest. The institution of interest also results in accumulating wealth in comparatively fewer hands. It enables people with established custom and connections to go on multiplying their wealth practically without limit to the detriment of the rest of the community. Those of you, who are engaged in agriculture, can realise full well how a portion of the earnings of a peasant finds its way into the coffers of the money-lender. Under an economic system which could have made provision for agricultural credit on some basis other than that of interest, the peasantry in this country would have been very much more prosperous than it is today. Under the system now prevalent once a peasant is compelled to borrow, all his savings are absorbed by interest on the loan, and even after he has repaid the amount of the loan, many times over in the shape of interest, the original loan still remains due from him. Interest is, therefore, a curse which like a leech goes on sucking the blood of the poor. If the world desires economic peace, interest must be abolished, so that wealth is not permitted by this means to be monopolized by a small section of the community.

It may be urged that the three principles to which I have so far made reference no doubt secure that property and wealth should be continuously divided and sub-divided, and money should be put into circulation so as to prevent its accumulation in a few hands, but they make no provision for the direct relief of poverty and distress. The answer is that Islam supplements these with a fourth principle by providing for compulsory levies and encouraging voluntary contributions for the relief of poverty. Under the institution of Zakat, it is the duty of an Islamic State to levy a tax of 2½% on average upon all wealth and capital which has been in the possession or under the direction of an assessee for one year. The proceeds of this tax must be devoted exclusively towards the relief of poverty and the raising of the standard of living of the poor. It must be noted that this tax is to be levied not merely upon the income or profits, but on capital and accumulations, so that sometimes this 2½% may amount to as much as 50% of the income or profits, and in the case of accumulations has to be paid out of the accumulated money. This also has the effect of encouraging investment, for, if a person has a certain amount of money accumulated in his hands or lying to his credit, he will have to pay Zakat on it at the rate of 2½% per annum, so that gradually the money will begin to disappear in payment of the tax. Every normal person, therefore, is compelled to invest his money and to put it into circulation so that he may be able to meet the assessment out of the profit earned. This results in a double benefit to the community as it secures the circulation of wealth and thus provides employment for all sections and in addition secures 2½% of the capital and the profits made for the benefit of the poor. Under the stress of war conditions many people in this country are beginning foolishly to hoard gold and silver with the result that the prices of these metals have risen very high. The poorer sections are being forced to part with what little of these precious metals they may have accumulated in order to provide for their daily needs, and sometimes merely because they are tempted by the high prices which at present rule the market. On the other hand, these metals are being hoarded by bankers, money-lenders and others who fear that in the case of a Japanese invasion of the country, currency notes would become valueless. They do not realise that in the event of a successful Japanese invasion they will be deprived of all their accumulated gold and silver. Whatever the reason, the price of gold and silver is being forced up and poorer sections of the people have had to part with even the small quantities of these metals which they had accumulated in the past. The Islamic economic system, however, recommends that money and wealth should be constantly in circulation and employed in the service of the community, and that all accumulations, capital and profits, should be made to contribute towards the relief of poverty and the raising of the standard of living. If the injunctions, laid down by Islam in this respect, are obeyed and carried into effect, the most miserly person would be compelled to invest his savings and thus make a contribution towards general prosperity, and in addition pay 2½% on them towards the relief of poverty.

It must, however, be remembered that in spite of all these provisions, Islam recognises the right of private property and individual ownership. But it ensures that the individual owner should treat his property as a sort of trust and subjects the institution of private property to limitations and correctives which tend to reduce the power and influence of the wealthier sections of the community.

It may be asked, why should not the Bolshevik system be preferred to the Islamic system? The answer is that the object of an ideal economic and social system should be to bring about conditions of peace and justice and to promote the spirit of progress. The Bolshevik system brings about an upheaval by means of a sudden revolution which deprives at one stroke the propertied classes of all their wealth, and thus creates bitter resentment between different sections. To deprive a wealthy person of his house, property, money and other forms of wealth is bound to administer an unbearable shock to him and to plunge him into misery and resentment. The bitterest enemies of the Bolsheviks are the aristocratic Russians who have been deprived of all their property and privileges and have been driven out of the country in a penniless and destitute condition. I had occasion to see some of these Russians during my stay in Europe, and I found that they were bitter enemies of the Bolshevik State. The reason is that from luxury they were instantly driven into penury and privation. It is true that a large share of their wealth should have rightfully belonged to the poorer sections of the people of their country, but generation after generation these people had believed that they were entitled to the ownership of their estates and other property, and when they were forcibly ejected therefrom, their reaction was very bitter indeed. That is why the Holy Prophet of Islam[sa] has said that old established titles should not be upset; that is to say, people with such titles and properties should not be subjected to treatment which should make them feel that they were being cruelly treated.

Secondly, Bolshevism ignores the fact that intellectual capacity is as much an asset as property and wealth. It exalts manual labour at the expense of intellectual effort, and it is a natural principle that whatever is not properly appreciated begins to decline. Those who do not value money soon run through it and those who lay no store by property are soon left without any. In the same way, people who do not appreciate intellectual effort begin to decline intellectually. The Bolshevik system is, therefore, subject to the serious drawback that by failing to recognise intellectual capacity as a valuable asset it discourages intellectual effort which is bound to lead to intellectual degeneration on a national scale. The reason why intellect is not regarded as a valuable asset by the Bolsheviks is that they are unable to subject it to compulsory equal distribution and to deal with it as tangible property. As against this, Islam brings about a gradual change and transformation and secures by gentle persuasion the application of all manner of talent and property in the service of mankind. By this means it succeeds in procuring a distribution not only of tangible property but also of intellectual capacities. In this respect even nature operates in opposition to the Bolshevik system. Nature endows different persons with different kinds and degrees of intellectual capacity, and the Bolsheviks have discovered no method of bringing about an equal distribution of this asset. Islam secures an equitable distribution in this respect also by directing that intellectual capacities also should be devoted to the service of humanity. The Holy Qur'ān says:

$$وَمِمَّا رَزَقْنَاهُمْ يُنْفِقُونَ$$

And they spend of that We have bestowed upon them. (2:4).

That is to say, those who believe sincerely and are anxious to attain nearness to God go on spending whatever We have given them (whether by way of intellectual and physical capacities or by way of wealth and property) in the service of mankind. (2:4). Thus Islam secures a distribution of all kinds of capacities and wealth not by force or violence but voluntarily through persuasion. This method secures all the benefits resulting from a general application of all talents and property to the service of mankind and being perfectly voluntary it leaves no sense of bitterness or resentment behind.

In spite of its high-sounding principles, Bolshevism has not succeeded in bringing about perfect equality in practice. In Russia even under the present system there are differences between the high and the low and between the rich and the poor. The most passionate advocate of Bolshevism will not claim that perfect equality has been achieved in Russia in all respects. Surely a peasant in the country districts does not eat the same food as those in authority in the bigger towns. On special occasions state banquets continue to be held and money is spent lavishly upon them. Only a short while ago when Mr. Wendell Wilkie went to Russia a banquet was given in his honour at which, according to press reports, sixty courses were served and Stalin and other Bolshevik officials who were present must have partaken of them. According to Bolshevik principles every citizen of the capital, as a matter of fact, every one of the 180 million people of Russia, is entitled to ask that these sixty courses should be provided for them also. It will be said that this would be impracticable and that exceptions must occasionally be made. But this would apply all over the field. If exceptions must occasionally be made and some distinctions must be tolerated, why upset the whole of society in a futile effort to abolish all distinctions? Why not try and bring about an equitable state of affairs in a manner which creates no bitterness?

Another consequence which is bound, in course of time, to come upon Bolshevism is that the country will begin to lose the benefit of the intellectual effort of its best brains. When Russian scientists and technicians find that they can derive no individual benefit from their intellectual activities, they will begin to find excuses for leaving the country and settling down in countries where the result of their researches may find better recompense and appreciation and bring higher individual reward. This will mean that other countries will benefit from the activities of the keenest Russian intellect, but Russia herself will be deprived of them. This tendency may not be apparent at this stage but is bound to manifest itself later on. Bolshevik principles sound very attractive just now, as the country had emancipated itself only very recently from Czarist tyranny, but as time passes their practical deficiencies will begin to press themselves upon the attention of the people. Bolshevik principles are very much like the teaching of the Bible, that if a person is smitten on the right cheek he should present the left one to the one who smites. This sounds very attractive so long as it is not put into practice. But if an attempt is made to act upon it, it is soon discovered to be entirely impracticable. It is related, that a Christian missionary used to preach in the streets of Cairo how full of love and tolerance the teachings of Jesus were. He would cite the injunction to turn the left cheek when the right one is smitten as an example, and make unfavourable comparisons with the teachings of other faiths. His discourses were couched in a very fine language and his audience used to be greatly affected. A Muslim, who had heard the missionary preach in this fashion on several occasions, became much upset. He wondered why no Muslim divine cared to tackle the

New World Order

missionary on the comparative merits of Islamic and Christian teachings. One day while the missionary was in the middle of his discourse this man approached him and expressed a desire to speak to him. The missionary inclined his head towards him to be able to listen to what he had to say. But the man instead of saying anything gave the missionary a violent slap on the face. The missionary was taken aback for a moment, but then fearing lest the man should proceed to further violence, raised his own hand in order to strike his assailant. The man remonstrated with the missionary and pointed out that he was expecting that in accordance with the Christian teaching, the missionary, instead of preparing to strike him in return, would turn his other cheek towards him. The missionary said, "I have decided today to act upon the teaching of the Qur'an, not the Bible."

Some doctrines may seem or sound very attractive but prove entirely impracticable when tried out in practice. The same is the case with Bolshevism. There is great enthusiasm in support of it at the moment on account of its contrast with the tyranny of the Czars from which the country has only recently been rescued. Once that is forgotten, the natural desire to reap the benefits of one's labour and effort will reassert itself and the newer generations will begin to rebel against the system of dead uniformity which

Bolshevism seeks to impose, and all sorts of evils will begin to manifest themselves. As against this, the Islamic system, being perfectly voluntary and natural, never leads to rebellion though people may often fall short of its teachings in practice.

XII

A study of all these movements, however, reveals one feature common to them all: it is that the State ought to exercise a great deal more control over national wealth and sources of production than it has done in the past. Experience has shown that the old systems of taxation do not enable the State to provide an adequate system of relief and help for the poorer sections of the community. It is necessary, therefore, to devise new means whereby a more equitable distribution of national wealth should become possible of achievement. We may be asked what Islam has done to achieve this object.

I have already mentioned the institution of Zakat. But it may be asked whether Zakat by itself would be adequate in these days to provide food, clothing, shelter, medical attendance and relief for every member of the community? The only honest answer to this question will have to be that at the present day Zakat by itself would prove inadequate for the

NEW WORLD ORDER 101

purpose. The responsibilities of a civilized State have increased manifold in recent years. In the past, the main functions of the State were to provide for the defence of the country, maintain internal security, establish educational institution, hospitals and means of communication etc., and to embark upon beneficent activities the necessity of which may become manifest from time to time. The relief of poverty and distress was not looked upon as one of the functions of the State. This was left to private charity and enterprise. But private charity and enterprise have failed to make adequate provision for the purpose, so poverty and distress continue to multiply. It is now urged and is beginning to be recognised that it is the duty of the State to make adequate provision in respect of these matters. Islam has from the very beginning laid down this duty for the State. That being so, it must either be shown that the institution of Zakat can adequately meet these demands, or it must be explained what other provision Islam has made in this behalf.

This is an important problem and we must address ourselves seriously to its solution. Had it not been claimed that Islam makes the State responsible for adequate provision in this behalf, it would not have been obligatory upon us to discover the solution of this problem in the Islamic teaching itself. The problem would have been dealt with as a new social problem for which a new solution must be found. But the problem is as old as humanity, and we claim that Islam is the only religion which has essayed to bring about practical equality between the rich and the poor. It seeks to bring various sections of the community so close to one another that class distinctions should in practice disappear and all sections should be able to fulfil their needs with regard to food, clothing, shelter, health and education, in an adequate measure. That being so, the solution of the problem must be found within the Islamic teaching. If Zakat does not make adequate provision in this respect, we must be able to discover supplemental provisions in the Islamic teaching.

Socialism has sought to find a remedy for the present disparity in the distribution of wealth by making workers' share in the profits of industry and commercial enterprise; that is to say, it advocates that labour should be rewarded not by means of wages but by the distribution of a certain percentage of the profits of each industry and commercial enterprise among the workers. But this principle is bound to lead to various anomalies in practice. Some concerns may yield much larger profits than others, which means that for similar work, workers employed in one concern will be paid very much more than workers employed in another concern. This is bound to cause trouble. As under this system a worker's wages will be determined not by the quantity and quality of the work performed by him but by factors many of which will depend upon pure chance, very soon the more successful concerns will attract the more skilled and the more diligent workers and people will refuse to work in less successful concerns. It may be urged that under a socialist system a uniform level of adequate wages will be fixed for all workers. Even that would afford no solution as skill and enterprise in the management will enable some concerns to work more profitably than others, and in the case of the latter gradually the cost will begin to eat up the capital. The problem can be tackled only on the basis of competitive earnings by the exercise of skill and labour supplemented by a State system of relief wherever necessary. But neither of the two devices to which I have just made reference proceeds on this basis.

Another device advocated by Socialism is State control of all basic industries and enterprise like railways, mines, electric power, etc. But this also is open to various objections. In any case, measures of this description are likely to vary from country to country and the system lacks the element of universality. Some countries might succeed in eliminating want and poverty under this system and other countries may continue to suffer from them.

Each State will still be responsible only for the poor of its own territories. Again, this system also, would tend to discourage individual talent which, as I have tried to explain, leads to intellectual decline.

I am not familiar with the details of the scheme which National Socialism may have put forward or adopted for this purpose. I do know that in Germany a great deal of State encouragement is given to capitalists and industrialists who contribute generously towards the social services. I am not aware, however, to what extent the State makes itself responsible for individuals or whether by such voluntary means adequate resources become available to the State. In any case, the scheme leaves the State very much at the mercy of leading capitalists and industrialists.

The Bolshevik scheme is that all important industries and commercial enterprises should be run by the State, and all surplus wealth whether derived from agriculture or other occupation should be taken over by the State. I have already detailed the principal objections to this system. Briefly, it kills individual initiative and is bound in the end to absolutism. The French Revolution tried to set up a people's Government but only succeeded in producing a tyrant like Napoleon. Conversely, in Russia the Czarist regime produced Bolshevism which appears at the moment to be gaining strength but, in a short time, will produce a new absolute Dictator or Ruler. Again, it has engendered a considerable amount of class bitterness by persecuting the propertied and intellectual sections of the community. Islam sets up quite a different ideal before us. In the first place, it points out that comfort and happiness have not the same meaning as has been given to them in Europe and America. In those continents comfort and happiness are understood to mean luxurious living and methods of indulgence. The object of the different equalitarian movements is to provide all these for everybody. Against this, Islam seeks to bring about equality by prohibiting luxury and indulgence even in the case of the rich. It is true that the object to be aimed at is universal happiness, but Islam, while encouraging the pursuit of happiness, also desires to raise the moral standard, so that a striking difference between the objectives aimed at by these movements and that aimed at by Islam is that whereas these movements seek to spread happiness through luxury and indulgence, Islam desires to bring about equality by persuading everybody to adopt simple modes of living. That is why wine, dancing etc., are prohibited in Islam. In Europe when the poor sections complain of hardships, they point out that whereas they can get only a glass or two of beer a day, the rich are able to drink as much wine as they feel inclined to. This grievance is admitted to be just and the governments then proclaim that they will take steps to enable the poor of their countries to drink more wine and beer! Against this, Islam would say, 'Your grievance is just but the remedy is that neither the rich nor the poor shall be permitted to indulge in the drinking of wine or beer; for, this habit is injurious both for body and for soul.' Again, poor people complain that the rich have many facilities for going to balls and dances, while the poor are deprived of any such pleasure. The reply of those in authority is that dance halls must be provided for the poor also and that the rich must contribute towards this object. Islam would say that dancing leads to moral deterioration and that equality is brought about not by providing facilities for dancing for the poor, but by prohibiting dancing altogether, so that the moral standards of the community should suffer no deterioration, and true culture and civilization should rise.

XIII

So far, therefore, as luxuries and indulgences are concerned, Islam brings about equality by prohibiting them altogether. It is obvious that States and systems which seek to provide luxuries and means of

New World Order

indulgence for all classes are bound to embark upon exploitation of their weaker neighbours. As against this, States, which aim at uniform standards of simple living, have only to persuade the wealthier sections of their own people to adopt simpler standards. It is very much easier to enforce and maintain standards of simple living than to set limits to luxury and indulgence. The standard of equality aimed at by Islam is much more easily attainable than the standards which the European and American communities have set themselves. Islam can succeed in bringing about reconciliation between the classes in providing reasonable standards of comfort for everybody at much less expense than would be the case with other communities. On the one side, the object is to provide luxuries for the poor as well as for the rich, and on the other, the object is to make adequate provision for the necessaries of life for the poor and to prohibit luxuries and means of indulgence to the rich. Islam can restore peace and comfort to mankind with much less effort and expense than is possible, for instance, for Christianity. Islam prohibits the wearing of silk by men; it prohibits eating and drinking out of vessels of gold and silver; it prohibits the erection of stately buildings for the sake of pomp and show. Similarly, it prohibits Muslim women from spending large sums upon ornaments. It makes the drinking of wine, gambling and betting unlawful. The object of these prohibitions is to enforce simple standards of living among the rich so that they can be persuaded to contribute their surplus for the relief of the poor. On the other hand, the poor would have no desire to indulge in these luxuries as they will have no temptation to imitate the rich in respect of them.

Again, Islam provides scope for individual effort, encourages it and seeks to induce the rich by persuasion and moral exhortation to make voluntary contributions towards the relief of the poor. I have already pointed out the injurious results that are bound to flow from the suppression or discouragement of individual effort and initiative and also those that are bound to result from violent and compulsory dispossession. Universal peace, comfort and happiness can be secured only under a system which keeps alive individual effort and initiative and secures adequate means for the relief of the poor by persuasion. This is what Islam aims at. Other movements generally advocate compulsory acquisition of all surplus wealth. But apart from the recovery of compulsory taxes, Islam does not permit compulsory acquisition. It proceeds by the method of persuasion which results in an increase of goodwill and affection between the different sections. If a rich man is deprived compulsorily of his surplus wealth, he is not likely to feel much affection towards those for whose benefit he has been so deprived, nor will the poor under such a system have any particular feelings of gratitude or affection for the rich. If, on the other hand, a person voluntarily devotes his surplus wealth towards the service of humanity, he is bound to be inspired by feelings of benevolence and affection towards others, while those who derive benefit from the application of his wealth to their service are bound to hold him in esteem and affection. This method is calculated to promote universal goodwill between different sections of mankind.

The encouragement of individual effort will ensure that everybody will follow his own particular pursuit or occupation with diligence, and this must result in continuous intellectual progress. A physician will try to achieve the highest success in the art of healing, an engineer will aim at getting ahead of fellow professionals in his particular branch of engineering, a manufacturer will try to improve his methods so as to secure the highest yield at the lowest cost and so on. If each of them is further persuaded to contribute generously towards the service of their fellow-beings, the necessary funds will be secured while maintaining intellectual progress, and without occasioning any resentment or bitterness. Bolshevism, as I have said, tends to arrest intellectual progress and the method of compulsion employed by it creates bitterness in the hearts of those who are dispossessed of their property. Against this, if everybody is permitted and encouraged to exercise his particular talent to the utmost extent, a physician in the art of healing, a lawyer in the courts of justice, an engineer in the thousand and one activities that require the exercise of his skill, and they are then asked voluntarily to contribute out of their surplus towards the relief of their less fortunate brethren, they will experience no feelings of injustice or bitterness, but feel satisfaction and happiness of being able to serve the cause of humanity. This would maintain justice and fair-dealing and promote benevolence and goodwill all round.

Contrast with this the feelings of a person whose earnings or property are taken away from him compulsorily by the State. He will experience no surge of benevolence towards the poor. In fact, a sense of injustice will always rankle in his mind and he will always be ill-disposed and disaffected towards a system which constantly subjects him to such treatment. On the other hand, the poor will have no feelings of gratitude in the matter. They will be disposed to imagine that the mere fact of a man being rich showed that he had been unjust and dishonest and that it was a good thing that he had been compulsorily deprived of his surplus property. Under a voluntary system, a rich man will contribute towards the relief

NEW WORLD ORDER

of the poor, but there will be no feeling of injustice on the one side or hostility on the other. These will be replaced by benevolence and goodwill.

This is the method adopted by Islam. It imposes taxes for this purpose by way of Zakat and 'Ushar, and then supplements them by the injunction:

وَاَنْفِقُوْا فِیْ سَبِیْلِ اللهِ وَلَا تُلْقُوْا بِاَیْدِیْکُمْ اِلَی التَّهْلُکَةِ ۚ وَاَحْسِنُوْا ۚ اِنَّ اللهَ یُحِبُّ الْمُحْسِنِیْنَ۞

And spend in the way of Allah and do not expose yourself to destruction with your own hands, and do good to others, surely Allah loves the doers of good. (2:196)

That is to say, in addition to compulsory taxes you must make voluntary contribution towards the relief of the poor, and must not by failing in this duty provide for your destruction. This means that those, who have a surplus of wealth, will suffer no real loss by contributing towards the relief of the poor, but that if they do not do so, they will in the end themselves be destroyed. This verse clearly tells of the fate of the French and Russian aristocrats. Failure by the rich voluntarily to discharge this obligation is bound in the end to entail their own destruction. The common people would rise and destroy everything in their blind rage. In the language of Shāhpur district they would "say the final prayers" over the wealth of the rich. Our Khalīfatul Masīḥ, the First, used to explain this as meaning that in the Shāhpur district, the peasants go on borrowing from the money-lender and their indebtedness increases steadily until the whole tract becomes heavily indebted and all their earnings are appropriated by the money-lender towards the interest due on the loans. When this stage is reached some big landlord in the locality collects the peasants together and inquires from them what the amount of their indebtedness is. Each specifies the amount due from him, and the landholder then inquires whether they have any means or hope of repaying. Everybody expresses his inability to do so. It is then proposed that the matter should be settled by "saying final prayers." All of them pray and arming themselves with various weapons proceed to the house of the money-lender, put him to death and burn all his papers and books.

In this verse God enjoins that those who have surplus means should employ them in the service of humanity and should thus save themselves from destruction. In other words, Islam permits the acquisition of wealth by proper means but forbids storing it up, as this would ultimately lead to revolution and destruction of property. The verse then proceeds to say:

'And do good to others.'

That is to say, it exalts Muslims to go a step

further by reducing their own requirements and spending the money thus saved in the service of humanity. It enjoins, however, that this should be done cheerfully and not out of the fear that surplus wealth be destroyed otherwise. The object should be to win the pleasure of God. If this teaching is followed in order to win the pleasure of God, it would afford happiness to the poor, safeguard the rich, and win divine pleasure for them. The verse concludes:

'Surely Allah loves the doers of good?'

That is, you should not imagine that in acting upon this teaching you are being deprived of the wealth that you have lawfully earned. This would, in turn, prove a profitable investment which would win for you the Love of God, improve society in this world, and secure reward for you in the next. In other words, you will secure comfort and happiness both here and the Hereafter. This teaching safeguards individual effort and enterprise on the one hand, and secures the uplift of the whole of society on the other, the latter being also the declared object of Bolshevism.

It may be said: "This is very well as a teaching, but what we want to know is whether Islam has ever succeeded in providing food, clothing, shelter, medical relief and means of education for the poor. If it has ever succeeded in securing these conditions, we should be told how the system worked in practice." In answer to this, it is important to realise in the first place that only that teaching can be successful which is able to deal with conditions arising in each succeeding age. It should possess enough elasticity to be able to achieve the ideal which it sets before us according to the circumstances of each age. An absolutely fixed and rigid system may prove beneficent at one time, or in one place, but may cease to be of any use at another time or another place. It must be able to adjust itself to the changing circumstances of human life. By elasticity, however, I mean elasticity in application, not in principles and ideals.

In the early days of Islam, the social and economic teachings of Islam proved fully equal to the demands made upon it. The Holy Prophet[sa] not only insisted upon simple modes of living but as soon as Muslims achieved political power, history bears witness that the needs of the poor were fulfilled from Zakat supplemented by voluntary subscriptions. In this connection the Companions[ra] of the Holy Prophet[sa] used often to make great sacrifices. Ḥaḍrat Abū Bakr[ra] on one occasion contributed the whole of his property and on another Ḥaḍrat 'Uthmān[ra] contributed almost the whole of his belongings, so that in accordance with this teaching the needs of the people were fulfilled according to the requirements of the age.

When during the time of the Khalīfas the boundaries of the Islamic State became wider, the needs of the poor were fulfilled in a more organised manner. In the time of Ḥaḍrat 'Umar[ra] regular records were maintained of the whole population and the necessities of life were provided for everybody according to fixed scales. In this way, everybody, rich or poor, was adequately provided for, and the means adopted were suited to the circumstances of those time. People are apt to imagine that the principle of providing the necessaries of life for every individual has been invented by the Bolsheviks. This is incorrect. This principle was laid down by Islam and was given effect to in an organised manner in the time of Ḥaḍrat 'Umar[ra]. Under the scheme originally introduced by Ḥaḍrat 'Umar[ra], a breast-fed child did not qualify for any relief. The treasury became liable to provide relief for a child only after it had been weaned. In one case a mother weaned her child prematurely in order to be able to draw an allowance in respect of it from the treasury. Ḥaḍrat 'Umar[ra] was going his rounds one evening when he heard a child crying in a hut. 'Umar[ra] went in and inquired why the child was crying. Said the mother, "'Umar[ra] has made a law that an allowance can be drawn for a child only when he has been weaned. I have stopped suckling the child to draw an allowance on his behalf; so, that is why he is crying." Hadrat 'Umar[ra]—and he himself related this incident—says that on hearing this, he blamed himself strongly lest by laying down this rule he may have interfered seriously with the physical growth of the next generation. He immediately issued a direction that an allowance should be payable in respect of every child as soon as born. This was the arrangement in 'Umar's[ra] time and again it was quite adequate having regard to the circumstances at that time. It is true that at that time the gulf between riches and poverty was not as wide as it is today. Zakat, voluntary contributions made to the State for the purpose, and private charity, these three afforded adequate and timely relief to the poor. There was no industrialization, and commercial competition was not as keen as it is in modern times. Powerful States did not exploit weaker States as they do today. The system that proved adequate in those times would prove inadequate and ineffective today. But this does not detract from the excellence of the Islamic teaching on the subject. At that time the object of this teaching could be fulfilled by means of Zakat and voluntary contributions, and it did not become necessary to have recourse to anything further. Today Zakat and voluntary contributions do not seem to suffice and some thing more is called for.

NEW WORLD ORDER

Today the world has become much more organised, and States are being daily driven to the adoption of policies which should give them greater and greater control over national wealth. If any of the movements to which I have drawn attention becomes supreme, the necessary result would be that individual wealth will be reduced and the greater part of the national wealth will come under the control of the State. The countries in which the successful movements originated and those allied with them may attain to greater happiness and peace, but other countries will be exploited and will be faced with greater misery and suffering.

XIV

Evidently, therefore, the means adopted in the time of the Holy Prophet[sa] and the schemes put into force by the first four Khalīfas (Caliphs) to give practical effect to the Islamic social and economic teachings, will not prove adequate today. It is necessary, therefore, that in this age Islamic teachings should be given a practical shape which, while safeguarding against the defects which I have pointed out in the other movements, should succeed in placing sufficient resources in the hands of those responsible for putting the Islamic principles into force to enable them to bring about conditions of equal opportunity for all and to provide for the legitimate needs of the people. The Khalīfas (Caliphs) interpreted and gave practical effect to the teachings of Islam in this respect according to the needs of their time. As I have indicated, there used to be a regular census in the time of Ḥaḍrat 'Umar[ra] and a record was kept of every individual. The Islamic treasury was responsible for the legitimate needs of every person. Originally, this system applied only to those who were capable of bearing arms, but Ḥaḍrat 'Umar[ra] recognised that the responsibility of the State extended to other people also. Eventually, provision was made for all deserving persons out of the treasury.

In short, the Khalīfas (Caliphs) gave effect to the Islamic teachings according to the circumstances of their time. Today human life and society have become much more complex, so a new system is called for to give effect to that teaching. For the establishment of the new system it was inevitable that some one, raised by God, should inaugurate a New Order to put an end to the pains and miseries of mankind, an Order not of man, but of Heaven, one really equal to the needs of the poor and able to restore peace and contentment to all mankind. Every person, who believes that the Holy Prophet[sa] had prophesied the advent of a Messiah[as] and Mahdi[as], must admit that it was the function of the Promised One[as] to find a remedy for the disorder, unrest and misery from which the world is suffering today. That remedy should not suffer from the defects from which Bolshevism, Socialism and National Socialism suffer. It should make it possible to provide food, clothing, shelter, medical relief and means of education for everybody and yet safeguard mankind against intellectual deterioration, the discouragement of individual enterprise and effort, and tyranny and exploitation of one people by another. In other words, it should secure peace and goodwill between nations and classes, and also succeed in finding resources to fulfil the needs of all individuals.

It was, therefore, the duty of the Khātamul-Khulafā'[*] to devise a scheme in accordance with Islamic teachings which should prove adequate to the needs of the time and put an end to the miseries from which the world is suffering. As I shall presently show, he did succeed under Divine Command in devising such a scheme.

I have already explained that the essentials of the Islamic social and economic system are: (1) that the needs of all human beings should be provided for; (2) that in trying to achieve the first object the incentive behind individual effort and enterprise should not be

---

[*] i.e. the Promised Messiah and Mahdi[as], the greatest of the Successors of the Holy Prophet[sa] to come in the Latter days.

weakened; (3) that the system devised should be voluntary and should not involve forcible dispossession or confiscation; and (4) that the system should not be confined to one country or one nation, but should be universal. All the movements that are being boosted today are in one respect or other limited in their application. They pertain to sections of mankind. The Islamic system is not national or sectional but universal. The Islamic teaching pays due regard to all the four factors that I have just mentioned. Any movement, that is based upon these four principles, is bound to prove more beneficial than, and to be preferred to, every other movement.

I shall now proceed to explain how this object has been fulfilled and how these four principles have been built into the New Order, the foundations of which have been laid under Divine Command and in strict accordance with the Islamic teachings, by the person appointed by God for the guidance of mankind in this age as a Deputy of the Holy Prophet[sa]. Bolshevism, Socialism and National Socialism have all come into being after the Great War of 1914—18. Hitler, Mussolini and Stalin have all risen to power after the last war. All these new movements, which claim to have devised new plans for the relief of mankind, arose out of the conditions of 1919—21. The appointed one of God, however, laid the foundations of the New Order in 1905 in his *Al-Waṣiyyat*.

NEW WORLD ORDER

The principle was laid down in the Qur'an in the verse 2:196. In this verse no definite rules were laid down in respect of voluntary contributions. Muslims had only been warned that in addition to Zakat they would have to pay other taxes and make other contributions, but the quantum of the taxes and the form which they were to take was not prescribed. If at one time the Islamic State was in need of one percent of the nation's wealth, the Khalīfah had only to announce that the State was in such need, and that Muslims should contribute so much. If at any other time the State required two percent, the Khalīfah asked Muslims to contribute that amount. The Holy Prophet[sa] used to ask for voluntary contributions from time to time. The Khalīfas gave effect to the Islamic teachings by reserving a large portion for the needs of the poor out of the tributes that were received for distribution among the armies. The soldiers were asked voluntarily to give up a portion of what was due to them to be devoted to the relief of the poor. The Promised Messiah[as] has interpreted the Islamic teachings according to the needs of the present age. If the Islamic State has to provide food, clothing, shelter, medical relief and means of education to everybody, it must have at its disposal very much larger resources than would have sufficed in the early days of Islam. The Promised Messiah[as] therefore, announced under

Divine Command that God had ordained that those, who desired to win real Paradise today, must volunteer from 1/10th to 1/3rd of their properties and belongings. He went on to prescribe that the properties obtained by this means would be devoted towards strengthening the foundations of Islam by means of propagation of the teachings of the Qur'ān, the spread of Islamic literature and the setting up of Islamic missions. (*Al-Waṣiyyat*, Condition No. 2).

He also said, "Every matter that is connected with the strengthening and propagation of Islam, into the details of which it would be premature to enter just now, will be accomplished by means of the properties so obtained." (ibid).

That is to say, this money would be spent in the achievement of everything which is essential for putting into force Islamic teachings and giving effect to them. He indicated that it was premature to describe these matters in detail, but that somebody else would go into their detailed exposition when the time comes.

This is the Order which was set up by the Promised Messiah[as]. He has stated clearly that every matter which pertains to strengthening and spreading Islam would be provided for out of this money, but that it was premature to enter into details. This meant clearly that all the objects, which were to be fulfilled

NEW WORLD ORDER

out of this money, could not be fully explained at the time. Time was soon to come, however, when the world was to cry out for a New Order. From every quarter voices were to be raised announcing New Orders. Russia would claim to give the world a New Order. England would put forward a New Order. Germany and Italy would announce a New Order. America would proclaim a New Order. At that time a successor of the Promised Messiah[as] would announce from Qādiān: 'The New Order has already been set out in *Al-Waṣiyyat*.' If the world desires to proceed along the path of peace and prosperity, the only way to it is to put into effect the New Order set out in *Al-Waṣiyyat*.'

The Promised Messiah then says, "These funds will also be devoted towards securing the welfare of the orphans and the needy who do not possess adequate means of subsistence." (*ibid*).

Further on he says, "It will be permissible for the Anjuman, (i.e., the Association administering these funds), to increase these funds through commercial investments" (*op. cit.* Appendix, Condition 9). That is to say, it would be proper for the Anjuman, after recovering 1/10th or 1/8th or 1/5th or 1/3rd of people's properties from them, to increase the funds at its disposal by means of investments. He goes on to say that the test of every believer is that he should participate in this scheme and should seek the special grace of God by this means. He announced that only hypocrites will keep out of this scheme. In other words, the scheme is voluntary, but is, at the same time, a test of your faith. If you are anxious to win the pleasure of God and to deserve real Paradise you must make this sacrifice. If, on the other hand, these things have no value in your eyes, you can retain your properties in this world; neither God nor the Movement founded under His Command has any use for them.

It will be observed that under the Bolshevik system people are dispossessed of their properties by force. As against this, the Promised Messiah[as] says that if a person chooses to leave the Movement at any time, property made over by him should be returned to him, for in God's Eye such property is unacceptable and should be discarded (*op. cit.*, Appendix, Condition 12). How great a divergence do we have here between the two systems. The secular system takes possession of people's properties by force and violence, but the system, which the Promised Messiah[as] advocates, is based upon voluntary sacrifice, so much so that if a man withdraws from the Movement any property already made over by him to the Movement shall be handed back to him; for, that which is unwillingly offered is not acceptable.

New World Order

This shows that the object which Bolshevism has sought to achieve incompletely through a bloodthirsty revolution is sought to be achieved by the Promised Messiah[as] completely by the promotion of goodwill and affection between the different classes. Bolshevism advocates that the wealthy should be dispossessed so that their belongings may be applied to the benefit of the poor. The Promised Messiah[as] according to Islamic teachings says that, having regard to the necessities of the time, people should willingly hand over substantial portions of their properties. He has asked for a minimum of 1/10th from every body which shall be devoted to the uplift of orphans and the needy and towards the propagation of Islam and the strengthening of its social and economic structures. Every Aḥmadī, who participates in this scheme for the sake of God, must volunteer from 1/10th to 1/3rd of his property for the service of Islam and humanity and execute a Will to this effect.

Even if the whole world were to join Aḥmadiyyat, still the Promised Messiah's[as] demand would be that those, who are true believers and desire to win the pleasure and approbation of God and to inherit His Paradise, should hand over from 1/10th to 1/3rd of their properties for the achievement of the ideals laid down by Islam. By this process a substantial portion of all private properties will be acquired for national purposes, and without any coercion or violence the Islamic centre will, in the course of a generation, obtain control over 1/10th to 1/3rd of all private properties, and this fund could be devoted to the service of mankind. Nor must it be forgotten that this system is not confined only to one generation. Each succeeding generation is required to make similar sacrifice. The system being based upon the desire of those, who wish to win the pleasure of God, would apply to succeeding generations as much as to the present one. The second, third, and fourth generations will similarly go on handing over substantial portions of their properties to the centre, and in the course of three or four generations, the greater part of private property will be placed at the disposal of the centre. Assuming that the Movement were to spread over the whole of the world and to comprise the whole of mankind, the inevitable consequence of this system will be that within a few generations people will have handed over the whole of their property voluntarily and with pleasure to be devoted towards social ends. As under this system individual initiative and enterprise will have been safeguarded, people will all the time go on acquiring fresh property for themselves and their children and out of this property again they will voluntarily surrender from 1/10th to 1/3rd for social objects, and this process will go on repeating itself and will at each stage augment the social resources. Let me illustrate this by a simple example. Assume that a man has only Rs.100 and he bequeaths 1/5th of it to the centre. When he dies Rs.20 will be contributed to the fund and Rs.80 will be given to his heir. If in turn his heir bequeaths 1/5th, Rs.16 more will go on his death to the fund and Rs.64 will go to his heir and in the course of 3 or 4 generations the greater part of this original amount will be transferred to the national fund. Far from necessitating the oppression and bloodshed which have accompanied the Bolshevik revolution, this system, if it were to be widely accepted, will bring about the desired revolution without any bloodshed or disorder. On the contrary, poverty will disappear, goodwill and affection will be promoted between the classes and, without damaging individual initiative and enterprise, the greater part of the property will be transferred to the national fund.

Again, this system will not be confined to any particular country or nation but being of a religious character will be universal. The socialists of England are naturally keen on a system, the benefits of which are confined to England. The Bolsheviks of Russia prefer a system which works to the advantage of Russia. But Ahmadiyyat is a religion and invites Russia, Germany, England, America, Holland, China and Japan equally to participate, in this New Order.

The funds collected by this means will not be spent in any one country, but will be devoted to the relief of poverty and distress all over the world.

In short, all these secular movements support and strengthen nationalism, but the Promised Messiah[as] has devised a system which tends to promote universal brotherhood. At present in Russia, a Russian is forced to give up his surplus for the benefit of other Russians, but under this system an Indian voluntarily contributes for the benefit of the whole of mankind, and the same applies to an Egyptian or a Syrian. This is a marked distinction between the New Orders which these secular movements are seeking to promote and the New Order based on Islamic principles.

Under the Russian system people were deprived of their properties by force. Many of them left Russia and began to agitate against the new order of things in that country. They felt no glow of pleasure or satisfaction after they had given up their properties to help the poor. When a Russian was deprived of his property, he did not rejoice, but went home in great distress and told his people that a tyrannical government had dispossessed him of his property. But under this New Order a peasant who owns, say, 10 acres of land and provides in his Will that one or two or three acres out of it shall go to the national fund, does not grieve as if he has suffered a loss, but goes to his brother next day in great joy and asks to be congratulated for he has been able to persuade himself to make this provision by his Will in order to win the pleasure of God. In other words, making this provision for the poor causes him no distress or regret, but is something which affords him intense pleasure and he hopes that others connected with him will be able to do the same, so that in turn he may be able to congratulate them. When he informs his wife of what he has done, she does not curse the people who deprive her family of a portion of its property, but experiences a wave of emotion in which joy and envy are mixed. She looks at her husband with a kind of longing in her eyes and says, "God has enabled you to do this but I own no property of my own and cannot make such a Will. Will you not transfer some of your property to me so that I may also participate in this scheme?" She continues to use all her powers of persuasion till her husband agrees to let her have a portion of his property so that she too can make a Will in respect of it. In this way, out of a further portion of the property, 1/10th or 1/8th or 1/6th is bequeathed in favour of the common funds. When the son comes home and hears that his father and his mother have both made such a Will, he begins to feel melancholy and says to his father, "May God spare you for long years to us! I have no property of my own. How shall I contrive to make this easy bargain to win God's pleasure? If you will let me have a portion of your property I too could do what you have done." If the father is very fond of him, he lets him too have a portion of his property, thinking that in the end the property has to pass to the son. The son makes a Will in respect of it, and thus another portion of the property is set aside for the national fund. If the father is not to be easily persuaded, the son nevertheless makes a Will that he will pay a certain portion of his income during his lifetime to the national fund and that if he should die possessed of any property, the national fund would succeed to whatever portion he may specify. In other words, it means that when his father dies and he succeeds to the family property, the 'Will' will operate in respect of it along with any property that he may himself acquire, and in this way yet another portion of the original property passes to the national fund.

We observe daily that when the State imposes a tax, those who are made to pay the tax feel oppressed and those, who go free, experience relief. The rich are annoyed that they will now have to pay more to the State, and the poor are happy that a little more of the wealth of the rich will be employed for their benefit. In our system it is the other way about. When the system was first instituted, it applied only to properties and thus affected the propertied classes only, but those for whose benefit the system was instituted felt no elation at the thought that the property-owning members of the community were to be taxed for their sake. On the other hand, they felt distressed on the ground that they were not allowed to participate in this system, the reward of which was God's pleasure and paradise. They approached the Promised Messiah[as] and requested him to devise some means by which they also should be allowed to participate in the system. Eventually, under divine direction he permitted them to contribute specified portions of their income for the same purpose. So that though in the beginning the system applied only to properties, at the request of those who owned no property it was extended to incomes, and thus a portion of current income, as well as property, began to flow into the common funds.

XV

In short, the foundations of the New Order were not laid in Russia in 1910 or in any other country, nor will they be laid in future after the present war. As a matter of fact the New Order, which is designed to bring comfort and prosperity to every human being and to safeguard true religion, was founded in 1905. The world is in need of no other New Order. This New Order is not based upon coercion or violence but upon affection and goodwill. It preserves the self-respect of man, fosters intellectual progress and promotes individual initiative and enterprise.

It would not be correct to assume that the money collected under the system can only be spent on the propagation of Islam. I have already quoted *Al-Waṣiyyat* to show that this fund is to be used for the achievement of several objects. The Promised Messiah[as] has stated that all plans calculated to promote the spread of Islam in the world would be fit objects on which to spend these funds. Only, it was premature to describe those plans in detail. This means clearly that many of these objects could be explained only in the future. When Islam is given practical effect and its beauties began to be appreciated, there will be several purposes on which it would not only be proper but necessary to spend money out of this fund. Further, the Promised Messiah[as] has drawn attention to the orphans and the needy and has pointed out that they also would be entitled to relief out of this fund. These words point to the Islamic social and economic system under which it is directed that food, clothing, shelter, medical relief and means of education must be provided for every human being. In the circumstances of today this cannot be accomplished by means of taxes alone. It is necessary that wealth and property should be devoted towards this purpose.

It may be objected that we are a small community and that it would be vain to expect that we should be able to give practical effect to the expectations based upon this system. To this my reply is that it is a part of our firm belief and faith that the spread of our Movement has been decreed by God. Under Divine Revelations and in accordance with Divine Promises we firmly believe that in the course of half a century, or a century, Aḥmadiyyat is bound to become dominant. We believe equally firmly that the system which was inaugurated by the Promised Messiah[as] is bound to establish itself successfully. Heaven and earth may pass but God's Words cannot go unfulfilled.

It is objected sometimes that the progress of the community is so slow that it is not possible to foresee when this New Order may become established. The answer is that a structure which is not raised on firm foundations soon falls to the ground. These hastily constructed social and economic systems which are being advocated today will pass away very quickly. The only system, that will endure, will be the one based upon the willing cooperation of human beings. The grass grows today and withers tomorrow, but the tree which has to yield fruit takes long to grow and then endures for long. As our community grows, this system also will grow with it. The Promised Messiah[as] has said in *Al-Waṣiyyat*, "Do not think that this is all fancy. This is the decree of the Almighty, the Ruler of the earth and the heavens. I am not worried over how all this property will be collected and how a community will grow up to accomplish all this in the strength of its faith. What I do worry about is lest, after our time, those who are put in charge of these funds should be tempted by their volume and should yield to such temptation and incline towards the world. So I pray that God may continue to provide this Movement with honest and faithful workers who should work for the sake of God, though it would be permissible that in the case of those, who have no other means of subsistence, an allowance may be made out of these funds."

In other words, he had no fear that there would not be enough to make adequate provision for everybody. He was convinced that large amounts of money and property would become available. What he was afraid of was that people who might be put in charge of these funds might fall into temptation and begin to appropriate these funds for purposes for which they are not meant, and leave unattended purposes to which they ought to be devoted. So, the Promised Messiah[as] has himself raised this question and given the answer. People say, where will all this money come from? He says it will come without fail. His fear is lest people should begin to love this money for its own sake. He is convinced that money and property will come by millions, so much so that no State—American, Russian, English, German, Italian or Japanese—will ever have had so much wealth and property under its control. He is afraid that this might lead to dishonesty. He, therefore, tells us not to worry as to how this system would be established, but to be diligent in making ourselves fit for it. He has assured us that large amounts of property and wealth will be committed to our care and that we should so train ourselves as to become fit to administer these funds for the true benefit of mankind.

Here I cannot help paying a tribute to the foresight of one who subsequently became my opponent. On the day the Promised Messiah[as] wrote out his *Al-Waṣiyyat:* he sent the manuscript out and the late Khwājah Kamāluddīn Ṣāḥib began to read it. Reading the passages which I have just quoted, he was overcome by admiration of the whole scheme and exclaimed, "All praise to you, O Mirzā! You have made firm the foundations of Aḥmadiyyat." Khwājah Ṣāḥib no doubt appreciated the implications of the scheme to some extent, but not well enough. A careful study of *Al-Waṣiyyat* compels one to exclaim, "All praise to you, O Mirzā! You have made firm the foundations of Islam. You have made firm the foundations of humanity."

O Lord, shower Thy blessings on Muḥammad[sa] and the descendants of Muḥammad[sa] and on Thy servant the Promised Messiah[as]! Thou art the Master of Praise and Dignity!

XVI

As I have indicated, however, this scheme requires time before it matures. It must await the years when the greater part of the world will have accepted Aḥmadiyyat. Our present income is not adequate even for the efficient running of the centre. God, therefore, inspired me with the idea of the *Taḥrīk-e-Jadīd* as a means of establishing a central fund which may be utilized towards the more intensive propagation of Aḥmadiyyat. The *Taḥrīk-e-Jadīd*, therefore, is a symbolic offering of faith to God indicating that, as time is not yet ripe for the universal establishment of the New Order based upon *Al-Waṣiyyat,* we proceed to construct a humble model of it by means of the *Taḥrīk-e-Jadīd*, so that pending the establishment of the system based upon *Al-Waṣiyyat* we should be able to utilize the funds obtained through the *Taḥrīk-e-Jadīd* for the spread of Aḥmadiyyat, and this in turn should enable us to carry on into effect, on an ever wider scale, the objects of *Al-Waṣiyyat*.

It is obvious that as Aḥmadiyyat spreads, the system based upon *Al-Waṣiyyat* will embrace wider and wider circles and the national fund will continue to grow. Things always move slowly at first, but soon gather speed and momentum. It is true that the funds collected by means of Wills are at present not very large, but as Aḥmadiyyat goes on spreading faster and faster, these funds will also grow. By a natural process they will go on multiplying, so that the day of the complete establishment of the New Order will come nearer and nearer.

In short, though the *Taḥrīk-e-Jadīd* had in point of time been inaugurated after *Al-Waṣiyyat*, it is, in effect, its forerunner. In other words, it is an Elijah to the Messiah of the New Order, and it proclaims the ultimate supremacy of the message and principles of the Promised Messiah[as]. Every person, who participates in the *Taḥrīk-e-Jadīd*, helps to foster the system of *Al-Waṣiyyat*, and every person, who does this, helps in the establishment of the New Order.

To sum up, the system of *Al-Waṣiyyat* comprises within itself the whole social and economic system of Islam. They are mistaken who think that the fund established by *Al-Waṣiyyat* can be used only for the verbal propagation of Islam. This is not correct. *Al-Waṣiyyat* contemplates both verbal propagation and practical establishment. It no doubt includes missionary effort, but it equally includes the complete establishment of the system under which the needs of every human being should be looked after in a dignified manner. When this system attains maturity, it will provide not only for missionary work, but will also help to abolish want and distress by making adequate provision for the needs of all individuals. An orphan will not have to beg, nor will a widow have to ask for charity, nor a needy person to suffer anxiety. The system will be a mother to children, a father to youth and will afford security to women. Under this system, not by means of compulsion or coercion, but out of real affection and goodwill, a brother will be eager to help his brother. Nor will such sacrifice be in vain. Every giver will be recompensed many times over by God. The rich will not suffer loss nor will the poor suffer privation. Nation will not fight nation, nor class will contend against class. The system will put everyone under an obligation.

XVII

I assure you that the New Order will not be inaugurated by Mr. Churchill or Mr. Roosevelt.

New World Order

Declarations like the Atlantic Charter will accomplish nothing. They are full of defects and shortcomings. New Orders are always established in the world by Prophets raised for the purpose by God. They have no bitterness against the rich, and no bias for the poor. They are neither of the East, nor of the West. They are the Messengers of God and proclaim the teachings which furnish the foundations of true peace. Today also, peace will be established only through the teachings of the Promised Messiah[as] the foundations of which were laid in *Al-Waṣiyyat* in 1905. We should all realize the significance of *Al-Waṣiyyat*, and remember the fundamentals to which I have drawn attention in the course of this address. These days, the advocates of Bolshevism are to be met with everywhere. I have, therefore, been at pains to explain the merits as well as the defects of the Bolshevik system and of the other movements that have risen in Europe in recent years. When you come across people, who advocate one or the other of these systems, you should discuss with them the merits of these systems on the principles I have tried to explain to you. I assure you that the advocates of these movements will not be able to meet the criticisms which I have urged against them. Peace can be established in the world only on the basis I have explained. Eighteen years ago, in 1924, I explained in my book *Aḥmadiyyat or the True Islam*, the fundamental principles essential for securing peace. This explanation was based upon the texts of the Holy Qur'an on the subject, and the disclosure was made by me under divine guidance. I may assert that during the last thirteen hundred years not one of the commentators has drawn attention to so important and fundamental a truth contained in the Holy Qur'an. I can claim with confidence that God vouchsafes knowledge like this only to Prophets and their Khalīfas. If this is doubted, I should like someone to produce a similar instance from the writings of other people.

Those of you who have already made Wills in accordance with the directions contained in *Al-Waṣiyyat* are participating in laying the foundations of the New Order, the Order which is to afford security for every person who participates in it, for his family and descendants. Those of you, who have participated in the *Tahrīk-e-Jadīd*, even though it may be only by means of prayers for its success, are helping to enlarge the system of *Al-Waṣiyyat*. The world seeks a New Order by destroying religion. Through *Tahrīk-e-Jadīd* and *Al-Waṣiyyat* you will construct a much better New Order while preserving the integrity of religion. But you must be resolute and go ahead, for whoever outruns others in the race will win. All of you should, therefore, make your Wills under this system, so that the New Order may come as early as possible, and the blessed day may dawn when everywhere the banner of Islam and Ahmadiyyat will be seen flying. To those who have already made their Wills I offer my congratulations and pray that those, who have not, may be enabled by God to do so, so that they may also gather for themselves blessings, material as well as spiritual. I also pray that this system may prove of such benefit to mankind that they should be compelled to admit that from this backward and ignorant village of Qādiān, shone forth a light which dispelled the darkness of the world and then filled it with the refulgence of true knowledge, which abolishes pain and misery, and makes it possible for the rich and the poor, the high and the humble, to live together in affection and goodwill. Āmīn!

GLOSSARY

Acre: A measure of land equal to 4,840 squre yards or 0.405 hectares.

Anna: An obsolete Indo-Pak coin equivalent to less than one English penny of today.

Brahmin: A member of the supreme caste of Hindus, especially a religious leader.

Kshatriya: Class consisting of Soldiers above Vaishya in Hinduism.

Manu: A renowned name in Vedic literature. Manu Shaster is a book of Hindu's religious Law allegedly given by Manu in 600 to 200 BC in Sanskrit. Some times it is also used for the first man like 'Adam'.

Maund: An Indo-Pak measure. One Maund is equivalent to 40 kilograms.

OM: Hinduism's name for God.

Pulā'u: Indian dish of fried rice cooked in meat or vegetable curry.

Sudra: The lowest cast in Hindu caste system.

Vaishya: Craftsmen or people related to business—a cast above Sudra in Hinduism.

ANALYTICAL INDEX

A
Abbasids and Slavery 60
Abū 'Uzzah 65
Abū Bakr[ra] 114
  monetary sacrifices of 113
Abyssinia 74
Afghanistan 33
Africa 79
  African Tribes 79
  East 81
  South 80
Aḥmad, Ḥaḍrat Mırzā Bashīruddīn Maḥmūd[ra] i-iii, vii, ix, xi, xiii, xiv, xv, 2-3, 8-9, 15, 41-42, 47, 99, 86, 139
  an incident in his life when a poor women came to meet him and how deeply he was affected by the plight of the poor 8-9
  his effort to uplift the morale of the poor and the downtrodden and their reaction to his advice 15
  his prophecies about Russian Bolshevism 41-42, 97-98, 99-100
  his warning to the League of Nations 85-86
Aḥmad, Ḥaḍrat Mirzā Ghulām[as], the Promised Messiah[as] ii, iii, vii, viii, ix, xi, xiii, xiv, 118, 119, 121-122, 124, 134
  deputy[as] of the Holy Prophet[sa] 119
  Khatamul Khulafā' (the Promised Messiah[as]) and the Divine scheme of Waṣiyyat initiated by 118, 119
Aḥmadiyya Muslim Jamā'at ii, v, ix-xi, xiv, 2, 117, 138-139
  an advice to, by Ḥaḍrat Mirzā Bashīruddın Maḥmūd Aḥmad 138-139
  and socio political changes in the world 2
  how the political changes are going to affect it and other Muslim communities 2
  Islamic-Aḥmadiyya solution for the alleviation of poverty and socio-economic ills superior to that of Socialism, National Socialism and Bolshevism 119
Aḥmadiyyat or the True Islam viii, 85, 138
Allah i, iii, xv, xvi, 59, 61, 62, 85, 111, 113
Al-Waṣiyyat vii, viii, ix, xiv, xix, 120-123, 132, 134, 135, 137-140
America see also under USA
  North 77
  South 77
Aristocratic classes of Russia and Bolshevic revolution 37
Art 78
Atlantic Charter 139
Australia 77
  appropriated by the British 77
Axis Powers 74

B
Badr, the battle of 65
Boers 80
Bolsheviks 16, 18, 20, 23, 30, 37, 44, 82, 94, 95, 115, 127
  raised the hopes of the poor in all countries 24
  seized power from Mensheviks soon after the Russian Revolution 18
  welcomed by European masses 25
  a summary of the theories of 34
Bolshevism xiii, 14, 20, 21, 22, 24-30, 34, 37, 42, 45, 48, 94, 96, 97, 99, 104, 109, 113, 119, 120, 125, 139
  a brief history of the rise of 16-18
  and Islam 93-100
  and Communism 23
  and England ii, 12, 24, 27, 28, 31, 44, 85, 123, 128
  and Europe 25
  and France 23-24, 27, 28
  and Germany 23-24

and Imperialism 26, 27
and India 24-25
and Italy 23, 27
and Lenin 16-18
and Marx 23
and religion 21-22, 37
and Russia 23
   efforts of to convert other
   countries to Bolshevism 23
and Spain 23, 24, 28
and the implementation of Marxism 14
and the responsibilities of state 18-22, 34, 100
and USA 24, 27, 28
and why it cannot eradicate poverty on its own 7-8
based on Marxism 18
believes in bringing about socio-economic change by means of sudden and violent revolution 93-94
critism of 18-23, 34-42, 93-100
defects of
i) forbids individual effort and a critique of this 34-36
ii) believes in bringing about change by force and violence rather than by persuation and a critique of this 36-37
iii) opposes religion and the adverse consequences of this opposition 37
iv) has opened the door to dictatorship and a critique of this 37-38
v) creates barriers in the way of intellectual development and a critique of this 38-41
vi) promotes class struggle 41
vii) when it begins to decline its fall will be sudden and will lead to chaos 41-42
defies the laws of nature 95
failed to bring about socio-economic equality 96-97
prophecy about the brain drain from Russia 97-98

the appeal of, for the British Indians and a warning to the Indians 25, 75
the cardinal points of — a summary
i) individual effort should be replaced by collective effort 34
ii) manual workers should be secured against want and privation 34
iii) purely intellectual workers should have no claim upon the state 34
iv) all surplus wealth should belong to state 34
v) state should have full control and direction over means of production 34
vi) education and training of children should be in the hands of state and not that of parents 34
vii) the movement should seek to gain universal acceptance 34
viii) the proletariat should run the government but only after they are properly trained and educated under the dictatorship established by Bolshevic revolution 34
the objectives of 18
economic system of, philosophy and principles (based on Marxism) 18-20
  1. the first principle and its explanation 18, 19
    from each according to his capacity
  2. the second principle and its explanation 19
    to each according to his need
  3. the third prinicple and its explanation 19
    the surplus belongs to the state 19
  4. the fourth principle and its explanation 19
    not only persons but goods, too, should be subjected to state control 19, 20

5. the fifth principle and its explanation 20
6. the sixth principle and its explanation 20
   for making the working of these principles offence rather than of defence should be adopted 20
   and individual effort 34-36
   and system of education 22-23, 34
   and intellectual effort and development—19-20, 35-40
   and Nazism, Fascism and Falangists 24
   and the IInd world war, consequences of the victory of, for the world 47-48
   reaction of various countries to 23, 24, 28, 31
   reaction to, of Germany, Italy and Spain 23-24
   the success of Bolshevism's prapoganda in Europe 25
   the view of, that education is the responsibility of the state in the sense that state should decide what kind of education can and cannot be given to its citizens; under this principle it forbids religious education at all levels 22
   worldwide Bolshevick propoganda 23
British 33, 39, 46, 47, 74, 75, 77, 80
Buhler, G 55

C

Cairo 98
Canan *see under* Cananites
Cananites
   treatment of, by the Jews 51
Capitalism/Capitalist viii, ix, 14, 103
China 40
Chinese 38
Christian missionaries,
   an episode cited showing that their preaching proves that Christianity is impracticable 98-99

Christian Socialism 53
Christian(s) 13, 29, 49, 52, 53, 56, 58, 98, 99
Christianity xiv, 48, 52, 53, 58, 107
   ally of the successful 53
   and disparity between the poor and the rich 51-52
   and divorce, the Roman Catholic view 53
   contrasted with Protestant view 53
   and man-made law 52
   and slavery 58
   and wars 52
   can in principle have no socio-economic programme 52-53
   Christian civilization 53
   Christian ideal, the true meaning and significance of 52-53
   claim on its behalf that following it the world would get rid itself of all pain and tribulation 48
   claims to be superior to other religions 48
   criticism of, 52-53
   Divine law a curse according to, and its implications 52
   every socio-economic system that works in the West is dubbed as Christian socio-economic system by Christians and their governments 53
   like a wax model which can be moulded into any desired shape 53
   love and Christianity, analysis and critique of the concept of Christian love 53
Church, the 29, 57
Churchill 138
Class 4, 6, 9, 11, 15, 21, 41, 102, 105, 138
   and Socialism 12
   working class, reaction of to their own suffering 11
Communism/Communists viii, ix, xi, xiii, 23
   See also under Bolshevism
Companions[ra] of the Holy Prophet[sa] 66-67
   and the treatment of POWs 66-67, 70-73

Conference of Religions, the 85
Czar 17, 18
   see also under Marx and
   Bolshevism

D

Dacca 38
Dayānand, Pandit 30
Delhi 10, 39
Democracy xiii, 10-14
   and the disparity between the rich
   and the poor 10-11, 14
   and the socio-economic
   responsibilities of the state 10
   initially most benefits of were
   confined to land-holding classes
   which had representation in
   parliaments 11
   nationalist in scope 12
   the objectives of 10-11

E

Economic and social disparities
   and humanitarian efforts by good-
   intentioned statesmen and
   industrialists 7
   and industrialism 6
   and injustice 3-5
   and the responsibilities
   of state 10, 11, 22, 25, 31, 34, 35,
   41, 55, 101, 117, 118
   and the rise of the living standards
   of the rich 6-10
   and the spread of knowledge 5
   Eighteenth century wakes up to the
   problem of disparity between the
   rich and the poor and the rise of
   democracy and other secular
   movements which claim to address
   the problem 10
   have always existed 3-5
   response to, of Islam 57-138
   response to, of Judaism, Christianity
   and Hinduism 48-57
   response to, of the present secular
   movements, 10-48.
   the general attitude towards,
   in the past 3-5
   the present change in attitude to 6
Economic Slavery
   various theories advanced to justify
   74-77
   first theory 74-75
   second theory 74
   third theory 75
   fourth theory 75-76
   fifth theory 76-77
      the teachings and the practice of
      the Holy Prophet[sa] in refutation
      of the fifth theory 76-77
   four shortcomings and practical
   defects of these theories 77-78
   Islamic response to the economic
   slavery 78
   i) every thing created by
       Providence is for the benefit of
       all mankind 78-79
       this rejects the doctrines of
       Imperialism, National Socialism
       and International Socialism
       78-80
   ii) reduces the power and influence
       of those who are engaged in
       accumulating wealth by
       exploiting natural resources and
       claims that the wealth thus
       created should also be used for
       the general benefit of mankind
       and imposes 20% tax on all
       such wealth 80-82
   iii) forbids all kinds of exploitation
       of one nation by the other,
       however, does not forbid
       cooperation between
       nations 80-82
       compared to European
       Imperialism 81-82
   iv) seeks the establishment of
       international peace 83-85
       without international security
       and peace it is not possible to
       have conditions necessary for
       national progress 87
Egypt 39
Egyptians 39

England 12, 24, 26-28, 31, 44, 85, 123, 128
Europe 3, 25, 38, 44, 52, 94, 105, 139
Extreme teachings of Socialism Bolshevism and National Socialism lead to mutual conflict and war, a brief historical survey of their mutual struggle for supremacy 44-45
the socio-economic consequences of this struggle for the world 46-47
The Economic Structure of Islamic Society viii, xi

F

Falangists 24
a challenge to Bolshevism 24
Fascism xiii, 24, 25, 27
and anti-Semitism 29-30
and imperialistic ambitions of 26-27
and industrialization 25-26
and Nationalist Socialist philosophy of 28, 29
and religion 29
and Roman Catholicism and the Church 29
apprehensions about Bolshevism of, and propaganda by, against Bolshevism by 25-27
fear of, that Bolshevism was being promoted by England, France and USA 27
view of that the spread of Bolshevism is a death-knell of its hopes and ambitions 24
France 12, 23, 26, 27, 28, 31, 43
Franco 24

G

God i, iii, xi, 5, 15, 40, 47, 49, 51, 59, 60, 62, 66, 70, 73, 76, 78, 80, 96, 112, 113, 118, 120, 122, 124, 125, 129, 131, 133, 134, 136, 138, 139, 141
Germany 23, 27, 28, 29, 44, 53, 85, 104, 123, 128
see also under Hitler *and* Nazism Germans

support of, for the socio-economic theories of Nazism of Hitler 28

H

Hamrā'ul Asad, the battle of 65
Heredity and environment, influence of, on the personal development of individuals 36
Himalayas 10
Hinduism xiv, 48, 53-57, 75
and *Brāhmins* 54-57
and disparity between the poor and the rich 53-55
and inheritance 55-56
and interest 55
and Karma 53
and *Kshatriya* 54
and Manu 54-56
and other races and followers of other religions 56
and socio-economic duties of state according to, 55
and *Sudra* 54-56
the exploitation of their rights 56
and the caste system and adverse consequences of it 53-57, 58, 75
and transmigration of souls x, 53
belief of, that each section of mankind (castes) must act and remain within a prescribed circle and thus cannot abolish poverty and remove social barriers 54-57
Brāhmins have the right to the wealth of Sudras, according to, 56
cannot give a just social and economic order 53
criticism of 53-57
economic and social consequences of the teachings of, and *Vaishya* 54
except Brāhmin, *Kshatriya* and *Vaishyas* the rest of the mankind belongs to the caste of Sudras, according to 56
followers of all other religions are Sudras, according to 52
its belief in Karma and

transmigration of souls implies that poverty is the necessary consequence of the deeds done in the previous life and hence can never in principle be eradicated 53-54
slavery a religious institution in 58
why Hinduism cannot put forward a new programme for the progress of mankind 54
Hitler 24, 25, 29, 30, 44, 120
alliance of with Bolshevik Russia in the beginning of the IInd world war 44
and Bolshevism 25-28, 44-45
Germany has exclusive right to rule the world, view of 30
his belief that Bolshevism not beneficial for Germany 25-27
his betrayal and invasion of Russia in the IInd world war and its consequences 44-45
no religion should be encouraged in Germany, the policy of 29
the confidence of that his views and policies would win the support of Germans 29
and socio-economic theories of, a summary 25
and his philosophy of Nazism 25-31
and the role of state under Nazism 25
believes in expanding German industry and commerce at international level, his program for this and reasoning behind it 25
believes that England, France, USA secretaly encourgaing Bolshevism 27
aggressive policies of Nazism will result in the collapse of the then dominant powers—England France USA—belief of 28-29
Germans should have religion of their own, the view of 29
all religions born outside Germany should be opposed by Germans, view of 29
a follower of Pandit Diyanand in his view about the superiority of Aryan race 30
Germans have the right to rule others because they are the most superior race according to 29-30
his persecution of the Jews generates from his general anti-religious views 28-29
see also Nazism
Hoarding money and property, the adverse effects of 91

I

Imperialism 26, 33, 79
and Bolshevism 26
and England 26
and Fascism 27
and France 26
and Nazism 27
and USA 26
India 23, 32, 40, 45, 46, 75, 77, 79
and adverse consequences of Russian victory, for 47
and likely benefits of the victory of the Allied forces in the IInd World War, for 46-47
influence of Bolshevism in 23
the likely adverse consequences of German victory in the IInd World War, for 45-46
Individual effort
the importance of 34-35
benefits of 109
the injurious consequences of the suppression and discouragement of 108
Industrialisation 26
and economic disparities 6
and the rich 6, 7
and the working class 6, 7
Industrialism
has aggravated the problem of disparity between the rich and the poor 7
the apprehension of the poor about 6-7
Interest (Usury)
an interesting episode concerning

111-112
  forbiddance of, by Islam 90-91, 111, 112
  harmful effects of 49-50, 90, 111-112
International Socialism xiii, 12-13, 78
  and economic and social disparity 12-13, 78
  based on Marxism 13
  claims to be universal in scope 12
  see also under Bolshevick, Bolshevism
International World Federation and Islam 83-87
Iran 40
Iraq 40
Islam ii, iii, vii, viii, ix, xi, xiii, xiv, xv, xvii, xix, 43, 48, 57, 58, 61, 62, 65, 66, 67, 68, 69, 71, 73, 74, 78, 79, 80, 81, 82, 83, 85, 87, 89, 90, 91, 93, 95, 96, 101, 102, 105, 107, 108, 111, 113, 114, 115, 118, 122, 123, 126, 132, 136, 138, 140, 141
  a summery of Islamic socio-economic principles and objectives 118-119
  admonishes to spend on the poor to please Allah 111-112
  and abolition of slavery 57-58, 59, 73
  and equitable distribution of wealth 87-90
  and freedom of faith 63
  and individual effort and initiative and its socio-economic benefits 108-112
  and intellectual progress 109
  and international peace 86-87
  and Islamic system of ransom of POWs 68-71, 74
  and marriage of POWs 67-68
  and means for securing improvement in National condition 86-95
  and prisnors of wars (POW's) 58-60, 64-68-71
  and prohibitions of certain things approved by the West 104-105
  and simple living 105
  and teachings regarding wars between Muslim states 83-87
  and a prophecy regarding the future wars 84
  the Islamic principles regarding how peace can be achieved between warring states and the system of international security 84-87
  and freeing of slaves taken in a just defensive war without ransom 64-65
  and the equality between the rich and the poor 105
  and the restoration of peace and comfort 105-109
  and the uplift of society 112
  and voluntry contributions 104-111
  contrasted with the view of the West 104-105
  creates equality between the rich and the poor by putting restrictions on luxeury and indulgence 105
  encourages voluntary contribution and socio-economic benefits of the teaching 107-108, 110-115
  happiness and comfort, the view of 103, 104
  involuntary and voluntary contributions enjoined by Islam need to be supplemented to meet the worldwide needs of today and in future, on the basis of Islamic teachings 116
  Islamic wars and wars of modern times 68
  raises moral standard of people 105
  the importance of this teaching and Islamic concept of comfortable life 105-106
  the philosophy of wars of, 61-64
  the significance and importance of the teaching of regarding wars 84-86
  the case of a POW who voluntarily remains with his master 71-73
Islamic response to socio-economic ills of the world 57-138
  four injunctions to eradicate socio-economic ills 87-93

   i first injunction embodied in the teachings of inheritance which stops accumulation of wealth in a few hands 87-89
   ii second injunction forbids of hoarding of money and wealth and teaches that money should either be spent or invested so that it remains in constant circulation 89-90, 91-92
   iii third injunction usury and interest should be eradicated 90-91 a clarification about the three injunctions 91
   iv fourth injunction compulsory levies (Zakat, *'Ushar* etc) and voluntary contributions 91-92 this encourages investment and checks hoarding of wealth 92 recognizes the right of private property and individual ownership 93 why Islamic system is superior to that of Bolshevism 93-100 Islam makes the state responsible for the welfare of the poor and the down-trodden 100 Islam's moral teachings promote the interest of the poor 109

the only religion which has essayed to bring about practical equality between the rich and the poor 102
three prerequisites for the alleviation of poverty 57-84
   i abolition of slavery 57-58
   ii eradication of all kinds of aggression 61
   iii a system for international security and promoting peace should be established 83 five principles to achieve this goal 84-85
see also under Economic Slavery and *Waṣiyyat*

Israelites
   see under Judaism
Italy 23, 24, 27-29, 44, 45, 74, 123
   feels that the spread of Bolshevism is a death-knell of its hopes and ambitions 29
   imperialistic ambitions of 24
   see also under Fasism
Ithkhān, meaning of , 59-60

J

Japan 42, 127
Japanese 38, 92, 135
Jesus 49, 59, 98
Jews 29, 30, 49, 50, 52
   support Bolshevism, the view of Hitler 29
Judaism 48, 49, 51, 52, 58
   and charity 49-50
   and Gentiles 51, 52
   and interest 49-50
   and slavery 49-50, 58
   and the harsh treatment of the non-Jews 49-51
   and the treatment of animals and the property of the people defeated in war, by 51
   and the treatment of the defeated enemy 51
   and war 51
   consequences of its economic and social system 51-52
   critiscism of 49-52
   descendents of Israel alone are chosen people according to 49
   purely racial 49-50
   teaches that poverty should be alleviated only among the Jews 50
   teachings of, not universal 49
   the rest of mankind created to serve the Jews, teachings of 49
   see also under Cananites

K

Kashmir 40
Kashmiris 36
Khadīja[ra] 72

153

Khalīfah 43, 115, 121
   the responsibilities of in respect of the implementation of the economic system of Islam 117-118
Khalīfatul Masīḥ[ra], the first 111
Khwājah Kamāluddīn 135
Krishna[as] 59

L

Lahore 3, 10
League of Nations, The 85, 86
   a warning to 85-87
Lenin 16-18, 38
   an orthodox follower of Marx 16
   and Bolshevicks 16, 18
   and capitalist society 16
   and death penalty 17, 18
   and his hatred for Czar 17-18
   and Marxism 16
   and the nature of differences with Martof 16-17
   and the proletariat 16
   and the Workers Organization 16
   carried on worldwide active propaganda among workers all over the world 16, 18
   first dictator of Russia 16
   gave definite shape to Marxism 16
   more orthodox followers of Marx than Martof 16
   the Czar must be put to death, the view of 17
   the nature of Government according to 17
   the propaganda of for the rights of workers gave rise to several anti-capitalist societies 16
   (*see also under* Bolshevism)
Liberalism 11
   and democracy 10, 11
   and state 11
   nationalist in scope 12
   serves the interest of the merchant and manufacturer class 11
Ludendorf, General and his wife 29
   and the ancient German worship of dogs 29

M

Manu
   forbids *Sudras* to save money and enrich themselves 54-56
   laws of 55
   and inheritance 88
Marx 13-16, 23
   a summary of his views 13
   a brief historical survey of the political situation in Russia after the death of 14-18
   advocates violent revolution to bring about socio-economic change in the world 14
   and Bolshevism 14
   and capitalist classess 14
   and Democracy 14
   and dictatorship 15
   and other political organizations 14
   and the capitalists 14
   and working classes 12
   critique of Socialism by 13, 14
   workers on their own cannot safeguard their interests, view of 14
   philosophy of 13-15
   political authority should be vested in the working masses only when under Marxist dictatorship workers are educated and organized and all class distinctions are removed from a society, view of 15
Marxism xiii, 13
   a development of International Socialism 13
   and political revolution 14
   advocates on the over throw of capitalists 14
   see also under Marx, Communism, Bolshevism, Lenin
Mensheviks 16
   the party led by Martof 16
   were the first to take power in Russia after the revolution 18
Missionaries, European 73
Moses[as] 59
Mecca 48
Mughals 56

Muḥammad[sa], the Holy Prophet 136
and *Luqṭa* (lost property) 76
example of regarding POWs 65-66
his[sa] teachings regarding the old established titles 93
Malatof 38
Mummies 39
Mussolini 24, 25, 74, 75, 120
invented Fascism to fight Bolshevism 25
and his philosophy of Fascism 25-28
and the role of state under Fascism 25
believes in expanding Italian industry and commerce at international level, his programme for this and reasoning behind it 25, 26
believes that England France USA secretly encouraging Bolshevism 27
aggressive policies of Fascism will result in the collapse of the then dominant powers—England, France, USA—belief of 28
Mughal palaces 39
Martof 16, 17
and the Czar 17, 18
and his differences with Lenin 16-17
views of, on the nature of Government and death penalty 17
Muslims viii, 40, 60, 62-65, 68, 112, 114, 121

N

National Socialism (Nazism, Fascism, Falangists) 42, 43, 48, 79, 104, 119, 120
and Islam 43
and Japan 42
and Socialism 42, 43, 48, 79, 104, 119, 121
Its defects
  i. aims at raising the standards of its own people at the expense of other nations, nationalists in scope 42
  ii. fails to provide spiritual peace 43
  iii. exalts the individual unduly as against the collective wisdom of the nation—carries individualism to the extreme 43-44
  iv. leads to conflict and endangers world peace 44
Japan, the latest follower of 42
an assessment and criticism of 45 and India 46
Nations, European 74-75
Nazism Fascism, and Falangists
their program for eradicating poverty 25-26
all advocate aggressive policies against Britain, France and USA with a view to appropriate the greater part of the wealth of the world 28
and imperialistic ambitions of all three 26-27
Nazism xiii, 24, 25, 28
and a call for a new religion 29
and anti Sovietism 28
and Bolshevism 24-25, 26, 27
and Christianity 28-29
and England 27
and France 27
and imperialist ambitions of 25-27
and Industrial and commercial classes 25
and Industrialisation 25-26
and international commerse with a view to exploiting other communities 26
and Judaism 28-29
and paganism 29
and persecution of Roman Catholic Church 28-29
and persecution of the Jews 29
and religion 29
and the right to rule over non-Germans 30
and the role of state in alleviating poverty 25
and the role of wealthy merchant

class 26
the state should take control of industry and commerce, the teaching of 25
and the superiority of the (Nordic) Aryan race 30
and the superiority of the German race 30
and the theory of Human evolution 30
and USA 27
apprehension of, and propaganda against Bolshevism by 24-28
Bolshevism not beneficial for Germany according to 27-28
consequences of the victory of, in the IInd World War 45
fear of, that Bolshevism was being promoted by England, France and USA 27
Germany, being poor, cannot achieve the aim of eradicating poverty and hence cannot adopt Bolshevik philosophy, must adopt teaching of Nazism 27-28
hope of that Natioal Socialist state established by Nazis would raise general level of prosperity much higher than could be achieved by Bolshevism 27-28
Nationalist Socialist Philosophy of, 25-28
overture to Russia during the IInd World War, by 44
religion is a source of strife and weakness, according to 28-29
view of, that increased commerce and industrialization is necessary to foster national resources 26
view of, that like England, France and USA, it was the turn of Germany to become imperialist in outlooks and exploit other nations 27-28
see also under Hitler
New World Order ix, xi, xiv, 86
always ushered in by the Prophets[as] 85, 139
and Russia, England, Germany, Italy, and USA 123
ushered in the world by the institution of *Waṣiyyat* 130, 137-140
Nordic Aryans 30

O
Om 48

P
Pārsīs 56
Pathāns 56
Poor, the 3, 5, 7, 8, 9, 18, 23, 26, 32, 42, 45, 54, 55, 74, 77, 88, 90, 91, 96, 102, 104, 105, 107, 108, 110, 111, 113, 114, 115, 118, 121, 125, 128, 131, 138, 139, 141
and their sense of deprivation 5
attitude of, to poverty 6
and feeling of oppression 6
condition of, in the past 4-6
attitude of the rich to 4-5
Poverty 6, 7, 8, 23, 26, 31, 37, 45, 49, 50, 54, 81, 89, 91, 101, 103, 116, 127, 128
Privatization of basic industry 103-104
Punjab 3, 23
influence of Bolshevism in 23

Q
Qādiān viii, 23, 140
Qur'an 40, 59, 61, 64, 67, 69, 78, 79, 83, 86, 88, 89, 96, 99, 121, 140

R
Rām Chandra 59
Religions of the World
except Islam, cannot usher peace and just economic order 57
teachings of, distorted by their later followers 56
see also under Hinduism, Judaism, Christianity, Islam
Rich, the 3, 5, 6, 7, 9, 18, 23, 41, 54, 74, 78, 96, 102, 105, 107, 108, 111, 113, 131, 139, 141
and economic injustice 6
and Industrialisation 6-7
Roman Catholicism—29

Rome —29
Roosevelt 138
Russia 16, 23, 29, 34, 37, 44, 85, 96, 98, 105, 123, 128, 132
  and the New World Order 128

S

Socio-economic and political changes in the world and how they affect the Aḥmadiyya community and other Muslim communities to be explained during the lecture 2
Slavery 50, 52, 57, 58, 60, 73, 74
  abolished by Prophets[as] alone 58
  and Abbasids 60
  and Christianity 58
  and Hinduism 58
  and Judaism 58
  and the Church 58
  not abolished by advanced civilizations 73
  the consequences of the abolition of, 58-59
  see also under Islam
South Africa 80
Spain 24, 28, 30, 44
  feels that the spread of Bolshevism is a death-knell of its hopes and ambitions 24
  imperialistic ambitions of 24
Stalin 38, 97, 120
Syeds 56
State 7, 10, 24, 39, 54, 63, 69, 71, 79, 97
  and Bolshevism 104
  and control of national wealth and responsibilities of, according to Islam 100
  and economic responsibilities of, according to National Socialism regarding the problem of poverty 103
  and Socialism 102-104
  and various secular ideologies 48, 128
  at present allows luxuries for the few and exploits the poor 105-106
  should own and be responsible for the improvement of national wealth 100
Socialism, International Socialism and the economic role of state 100
  the present day economic responsibilities of Islam 100
  the role of, in the alleviation of poverty through taxes 100
  and the socio-economic responsibilities in the past and the present 101
  see also under Bolshevism
Socialism 12, 13, 31, 42, 43, 48, 53, 79, 102, 103, 104, 119, 121
  active in England, France, USA 31
  advocates that workers should have share in the profit of an industry 102-103
  it leads to various anomalies in practic 102-103
  and amelioration of poverty 32
  and Imperialism 33
  and Internationalism 33
  and Marx 13
  state advocates privatization of basic industries and enterprises and criticism of this 103-104
  and religion 33
  and sources of national wealth 31
  and the cooperation with capitalist classes 13
  belief of that European interests in India should not suffer 32-33
  critcism of 101-102
  gaining ground in the most powerful and advanced countries 31
  has achieved the alleviation of poverty to some extent 31-32
  influence of, in England, France, USA 31
  its sympathies confined to respective countries—a secrat ally of imperialism—not universal 33
  nationalist in scope 12
  policy of that state should be given increasing role of controlling means of production 31
  purely secular and have no religious aspect and ignores the fact that

religions needs should be attended to more urgently than mundane needs 33-34
represents the working class—11-12
two serious defects of 33-34
Servant and Master relationship in the past and the present 4 5

T

Taḥrīk-e-Jadīd iii, ix, xiv, xviii, xx, 1, 2, 136, 137, 140
and Ahmadiyya Community 1
and human society 1-2
and the political economic conditions of the World 1
benefits and objects of, gradually dawned on the author 1
Divinely inspired 1
has a universal aspect which needs to be explained 1
importance of, not fully explained so far 1
objectives of xv, 137
paves the way for the implementation of the Institution of Waṣiyyat 137
the relevance of, to the New World Order xi, 137
the setting and the perspective of 2
to be explained in its proper setting during the lecture 2
why was the scheme initiated 2
will fulfil the objectives of Islam 1
will grow and strengthen the foundation of human society 1-2
Transmigration of souls xiv, 53
Travel and intercourse between nations, importance of, for the improvement of mind 38-41

U

'Umar[ra] 115, 116
and monetary sacrifices of 115, 118
practice and systematic organization of Islamic economic structure, by 115, 116

'Uthmān[ra] 114
and monetary sacrifices of 114
Uḥud, the battle of 65
UP, India 40
USA 24, 26, 27, 28, 31, 44, 46, 53

V

Voluntary contribution
benefits of 108-109
and Islam 111

W

Wars
the Quranic pophecy that a time will come when war will be denounced as evil 62
see also under Islam
Waṣiyyat
a glad tiding to the Ahmadiyya Community about the truths of Waṣiyyat and Taḥrīk-e-Jadīd—the last word 140-141
a summary of prospective achievements of 136-137
and Bolshevism 123-124, 127
and Islamic social and economic systems 132, 137
and New World Order ix, 131, 137-139
and secular socio-economic systems 126
and Tahrik-e-Jadid 136-137
and taxes, a comparison 130
and the response of the members of Ahmadiyya Community to 128-130
and the spiritual beauty of 127-128
answer to some objections to 132-135
based on four fundamental Islamic socio-economic principles (the needs of all should be provided for; individual effort should be encourged; the devised system should be voluntary; the system should be universal) 119-120
based on the verse 196 of chapter 2 (Al-Baqarah) of the Holy Quran 121-123

how the teachings contained in the verse were applied in early Islam 121
funds raised by, not meant only for the propogation of Islam but for all objects of Islam 132
on property (heritage) and on income 131
requires time to come into full fruition 136
supplements Zakat and voluntary contributions prescribed by Islam 121-122
the laying down of the New World Order, by 131, 137, 139
the participation of women and children, in 128-130
the scheme explained 120-122
the scheme initiated to meet the present day and future economic challenges, divinely inspired and endorsed by the Qur'an 120-122
the wealth created by, will exceed the wealth of the whole World 135
universal in scope 125-128, 137
Wendell Wilkie, Mr. 97

Z

Zaid bin Ḥārith 72-73
Zakat viii, xvii, xix, 61, 80, 91, 100, 102, 111, 114, 116, 121
and *'Ushar* 111
and voluntary contributions 111-113
dual benefits of 92
encourages investment 91-92
in early Islam, supplemnted by voluntary contribution, sufficied the needs of the people 114
not adequate for the economic needs of today 100-101
philosophy of 91
the reasons for 101
today more is needed to be done 117